UNFAMILIAR VENICE

UNFAMILIAR VENICE

By William Mathewson Milliken

THE PRESS OF CASE WESTERN RESERVE UNIVERSITY · 1967

To my mother,
"The lady who loved Venice,"
and
Bernard Berenson,
who encouraged me to write
these impressions

CONTENTS

CONTENTS

LIST OF ILLUSTRATIONS

LIST OF ILLUSTRATIONS

UNFAMILIAR VENICE

i

UNFAMILIAR VENICE

The present age has revealed a new aspect of Venice. To most people Venice is all; the lagoon is but a glimpse of water to right and left as they approach or leave the city by train or car. But from the air, the city instead is merely a compact point in the midst of variegated waters which extend on all sides to the horizon's edge.

The structure of the lagoon is revealed from the air, with changing pattern of shallows and waterways, their sun-warmed waters hemmed in from the sea by sandbars, the so-called *lidi*, green and silver in the sun. Over these waters the sharp breeze of a late summer day casts a net, a web of windswept ripples flecked with white, as regularly patterned as the enchanted sea upon whose waters Botticelli's Venus moves to greet her world.

The waves roll in upon the outer Lido shore and the surf leaves trailing points, fringing the beach with panicles of foam, like white wisteria drooping in cadence from wall or pergola.

Rainbow colors rest on the lagoon—pale blue and turquoise, lavender and palest rose, deep purple, green. In varying shades they reveal changing depths, the vagaries of underwater. No chart could give more clearly the twisting intricacies of the canals as they weave here and there amid the shoals, the *secca*, the land which twice a day appears above the surface of the water.

Human hand has had little part in the making of these canals. Man has only marked the more important of them by lines of piles, called *pali*, and has perhaps dredged them occasionally to keep them free of mud, as the sea waters move back and forth through the three great openings in the line of *lidi* which extends from Chioggia to Jesolo, forty kilometres in length. It is the mass of this water, rising and falling, driven by inexorable laws, which has made and makes Venice livable—the wonder of the tides:

> The moving waters at their priestlike task
> Of pure ablution round earth's human shores.
>
> (Keats)

And is that Venice itself rose and grey, so toylike, so completely patterned, or is it, rather, that engraving of Dürer's friend, Jacopo di Barbari, that ever-surprising print placed on sale in the year 1500 for three ducats? But where are the personifications of the winds blowing with puffed cheeks their carefully indicated blasts? No, they are not there, nor are the many strange and storied craft anchored in the Bacino di San Marco. Instead, a modern liner is at anchor, and a row of torpedo boat destroyers and of yachts is lined across from the point of the Dogana or Customs House. But the Basilica, the Piazza, the reverse curve of the Grand Canal, the broad waters of the Giudecca Canal are unchanged—even from this great height the Campanile seems the same.

> I leaned, and saw the city, and could mark
> How from their many isles in evening gleam
> Its temples, and its palaces did seem
> Like fabrics of enchantment piled to heaven.
>
> (*Julian and Maddolo*, Shelley)

Birds-eye View of Venice
Jacopo de' Barbari, woodcut

The Cleveland Museum of Art,
purchase from the J. H. Wade Fund

1. Upper left portion
2. Lower left portion
3. Upper central portion
4. Lower central portion
5. Upper right portion
6. Lower right portion

1. Upper left portion, *Birds-eye View of Venice.*

2. Lower left portion, *Birds-eye View of Venice.*

3. Upper central portion, *Birds-eye View of Venice.*

4. Lower central portion, *Birds-eye View of Venice*.

5. Upper right portion, *Birds-eye View of Venice.*

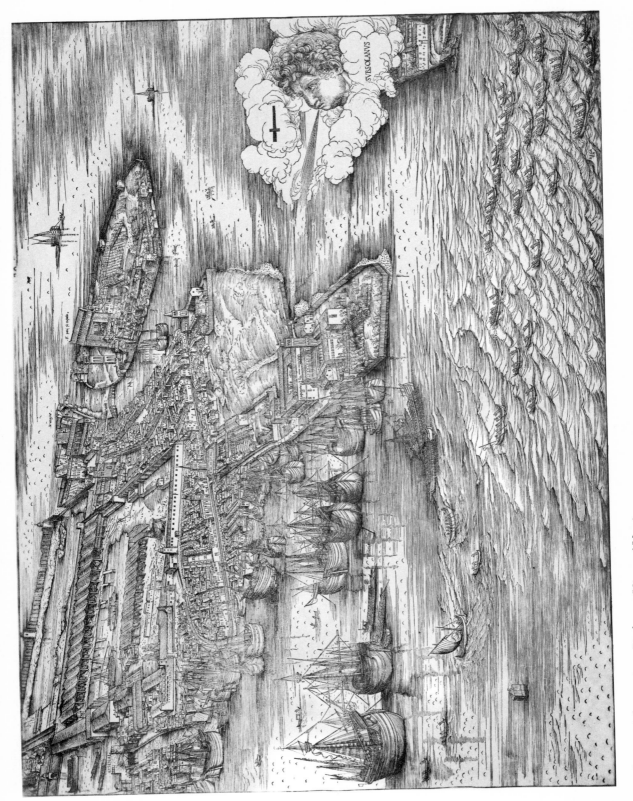

6. Lower right portion, *Birds-eye View of Venice.*

If with its vast spaces and changing tides the lagoon has insured health to the city which it surrounds, it has been the barrier, as well, which has kept Venice what it is through long centuries. Alone of Italian powers, Venice felt no conqueror's hand until Napoleon in 1797 brought to an end a depleted state.

The uncertainties of the lagoon were its own protection. The canals are marked by a few *pali*, which show the path to the fisherman amid a wilderness of shallows. A few *pali* gone, only the most experienced could find a way. The shoals are impassable. To be certain about this, it is merely necessary to see a fisherman at low tide wade with difficulty on the shuddering bottom, planting a foot carefully to withdraw it before it sinks too deeply in clinging mud.

High tide, low tide, the lagoon has a thousand moods. At high tide, beyond the Guidecca, the lagoon stretches in endless distance to a watery horizon line, fringed towards the sea by the *lidi*, which during the summer in late decades have become the haunt of a cosmopolitan world. On that side cluster the islands of San Servolo, San Lazzaro, La Grazia, San Clemente, and in front Sacca Sessola. The thin line of the mainland can just be seen to the north. The great rocky wall of the Alps beyond is hidden by summer haze.

Here in the quiet of infinite space the Venetian *popolo* love to come in their boats—*sandolo*, gondola, or *topo*—to enjoy the freshness of a summer evening, to plunge into the coolness of the lagoon, to dine *al fresco*.

As the tide rises, the islands shrink, the dark lines left by the outgoing tides disappear, the piles marking the borders of the canals shorten. The lagoon seems to be taking again to itself that which has arisen from its surface.

The tide falls. Can this be the same lagoon? No longer are there the great, simple spaces of water. Here and there the *secca* has arisen from the shallows to take command, the *pali* lengthen, the islands grow in size as reflection doubles their bulk. It is another world.

What a fascination it is day after day to follow the variations of the lagoon! the shoals rising from the water, the *secca* sinking, flecked with the white specks of the *gabbiani*, the gulls of the lagoon clinging like shipwrecked mariners to their last bit of security ere it sinks beneath their feet. Then they disappear in wheeling flight to seek other haunts until the tide falls and the *secca* gives them footing again for the time.

Here is the simple relation of man to nature which a more civilized but not a better world has lost—the intimate linking of the fisherman to the tides and to the seasons. For from the lagoon a host of simple folk wrest a meager sustenance.

One can follow the whole turn of the season here: the presence or absence of *gabbiani*, the running of the fish, the presence or absence of the *granchie*, the tiny crabs which infest the shoals. For as the season advances and the water warms, many seek their holidays in the cooler waters of the deeper canals. They have not learned the fashions of their human counterparts, who revel now in warmth, instead of seeking the cool mountains as they formerly did.

By July with its heat, the basket containers, called *canestri,* disappear from the edge of the lagoon between the canals of Santa Eufemia and Ponte Piccolo, where the larger canal leads from the Giudecca to Sacca Sessola. Until then the fishermen suspend these *canestri,* great baskets which might serve the purposes of an Ali Baba, from little *pali,* short poles driven into the shoals, so that as the tide rises or falls, the baskets are always suspended in the deeper water. In these watery prisons they store their catch, safely secured by inverted baskets of smaller size which close the mouth to any escape.

The fishermen start, ready for the propitious moment of the tide. Their boat, a *topo,* or its slightly larger counterpart, is filled with *pallini,* short stakes attached to nets. Some fishermen use tiny nets attached to single *pallini,* placing many of these so as to catch the fish which chance within. Generally, the fishermen prefer the long nets secured to *pallini,* which they cunningly set in a wide-flung enclosure to take advantage of the shallower water, so that as the tide falls, the fish are trapped and move automatically towards the main net set in the greater depths.

The boat is propelled by a single oar, perhaps by a young son who thus in early years learns the craft which will inevitably be his, while the fisherman himself leans over to thrust the pointed end with the net into the bottom or to withdraw it with characteristic motion from the clinging mud, when the catch is done.

The various sailing boats move smoothly with the wind, *barca a vela* with sails of rust and ocher, perhaps touched with green or ivory, with a variety of tones and patterns which wind and weather have blended. Back and forth they tack in the wind, the fisherman tossing out his net from the bow, sailing before the wind, drawing in his net from the stern, running forward, tossing it again. It is the day long, the year-long monotony of a craft. For the lagoon is good to them and from it they draw food and their livelihood.

After a rain or on a holiday, these boats can be seen moored to the *fondamenta,* the quay which lines the side of the Canal di Ponte Lunga. Their nets, hoisted to the top of their short masts, fall in graceful festoons punctuated along the bottom line by fringes of cork floats. Or the nets may hang in flounces along the *fondamenta* edge, supported by *pallini,* so that any rent can be found and skillfully repaired. Then the sails, half raised, flop lazily in the wind, or, thrown in careless abandon over the booms, instinctively achieve an effect a decorator would crave.

As the lagoons and the embarkations which sail them and as the *bragozze*—larger boats which go to sea for fish from Chioggia, Malamocco, and Burano—assure food for Venice, so the *lidi* and the islands to the east— Sant'Erasmo, Massorbo, and Torcello—yield the fruit and vegetables necessary for a great city. They are the garden spots from which come those products of the soil which, piled up in rich order, add such picturesque beauty to the markets of the Rialto.

Vegetation grows apace in the islands called *sacca,* or made ground, islands saved from the lagoon. Here are the subjects for a Guardi or a Canaletto—simple, homely subjects which under artists' hands become immortalized. And under familiar skies, their romantic pattern is repeated and will ever repeat itself. It may be only an island with shelving shoreline worn away, clumps of locust with leaves turned back, silvery in the wind, a wrecked house with tower and pointed windows framed in green by the hands of an ever-generous nature at just the points an artist would demand. They are the memories of time which has passed but which never really seems to pass in the timeless immortality of the lagoon.

Island lost in the wide waters, San Giorgio in Alga, your building of humble brick, arcaded with simple arches, tells the story of a religious life which is no more. From the corner of the brick boundary wall, a Madonna of marble looks forth across the lagoon. Water laps at the wall beneath her feet. A past century has placed over her head in dubious protection an *ombrellino* of copper, quaintly worked with pierced border of filigree. It is green with the delicious tone copper takes in the salt of sea breezes. On her head and on the head of the Divine Child perch in not-too-obvious security crowns of like workmanship, while tucked in the wall nearby, a marble St. George and the Dragon chivalrously plays guard.

But if nun or monk has long since gone, the Madonna has not forgotten and does not forget. The light which twinkles over the lagoon at night is

carefully tended, and bouquets of flowers or the dried grasses of the lagoon—
her lagoon, her kingdom—lie in humble tribute at her feet. There she gazes with
loving understanding upon the eternity about her.

Infinite peace spreads on all sides, the *passacaglia* of water as it slaps
against the gondola's side—the continuous bass of the sea, full of lazy
nostalgia. Chromatic figurations of effervescent waters caught by the wind weave
against this a silvery pattern, an infinity of variations on a single theme. The
sun permeates everything. Endless lines of *pali,* vague exclamation marks of
weathered grey which count as darks in the distance, pass beyond human
vision. In groups of three they punctuate the meanders of the canals like great
bunches of asparagus miraculously raised from the black mud of the lagoon.

There are moments of utter calm, when sky and water mingle
indistinguishably in opalescent color. Only the rust-colored triangle of a sail,
distant *pali,* an island floating double-fold upon mirroring water mark where
the horizon lies. The shelving shore of the island tapers to a point at either end,
and the reflected vision rises free from the surface of the lagoon like a great
dirigible. Winds draw suddenly a dark line across tranquil water and the
mirage collapses to become what it is, a bit of earth in the midst of the lagoon,
fringed with sedge, softened by the delicate foliage of dwarf locusts, the haunt
of sea birds. A faint ripple of wind upon the surface of the water, now a pale
green in the blazing sun, and the horizon line is marked again with sudden
sharpness.

Long Venice, James McNeill Whistler, etching. The Cleveland Museum of Art, gift of Mr. and Mrs. Ralph King.

ii

LONG VENICE

One of James McNeill Whistler's most famous prints, "Long Venice," emphasizes a characteristic of Venice which must have struck all who have penetrated beyond the inner periphery of the city—the impression of endless flat spaces with the long, slim line of distant sandbars, or the only slightly more substantial line of Venice herself. The choice of a horizontal plate and tenuous subject material doubly emphasizes Whistler's effect. Probably there was no other, deeper significance in the artist's mind than this simple recognition of one of Venice's most cogent characteristics, no profound analysis of the why and wherefore.

As the tide rises, Venice contracts. The sharp verticals of the *pali* and their reflections shrink, the reflected bulk of domes and palaces decreases, the oval of mirrored bridges flattens gradually, the broad, dark line of marine growth and incrustation along palace wall and *fondamenta* narrows and finally disappears. No longer does a sharp, dark pen stroke divide *fondamenta* and water. Venice seems to swim on the surface of the water: "Long Venice." The water almost reaches the *fondamenta* edge; the windows of the earlier palaces, gradually sinking into the muck of the canals—as all Venice is sinking a few centimeters a century—are not quite lapped by the rising water. The tides may rise and fall but little, yet the doubling of distance by play of reflection counts for much in a city where few buildings surpass three stories and where many are only two in height.

LONG VENICE

Venice at high tide is truly the "Long Venice" of Whistler. During
the high tides of spring, fall, and winter this normal condition is accentuated,
and if at such a time rain bathes quay and palace wall, where do land and water
end? Then, of a very truth, the lagoon seems to be taking back to itself at
long last the queen city to which it gave birth in the dark centuries of barbarian
invasion. Occasionally a combination of unusual circumstances may bring
such tides in other seasons, even in summer. A full moon, a strong wind blowing
for several days against the Lido mouth may be cause sufficient. Then the
lagoon does not empty as fully as is its wont, and the rising tide brings new
waters to add to those trapped within. Then the unwary merchant or householder
may find a basement filled with water, and if conditions do not improve, water
may rise into his main floor.

The bridges by San Moisè and one between the Archangelo Raffaele and
the Carmine are the danger signals to the gondolier, for they are the lowest of
all the bridges in Venice. Even a slightly abnormal tide makes the bridge of
San Moisè impassable, unless the gondolier runs forward so that his weight
permits the prow, the *ferro,* to pass through and under.

The water rises. The gondolas of the *tragetto* before the Piazzetta seem
to dominate the pavement in the rising tide. Slowly the water begins to trickle
over the edge of the *fondamenta.* Here and there barefooted gondoliers
carry their fares to the safety of dry land.

The water has already invaded part of the Piazza di San Marco. A hastily constructed bridge leads from the Ponte dei Dai under the Sottoportico dei Dai to the comparative safety of the center of the Piazza. There the *Banda Municipale* holds forth with the familiar beauties of Schubert's *Unfinished Symphony,* a prophetic title for such a night. Suddenly the lights flash out— the water has short-circuited the wires; the musicians play a few more notes, the music trails away, they gather their instruments and join the watching throng.

A few adventurous spirits sit at Quadri's, their feet on chairs, as they sip their espresso or their favorite drink. The waiters pick their way to them from chair to chair. Florian's is still perfectly dry, for that side of the Piazza is higher. The Procuratie Vecchie, beneath whose arcades the cafés Quadri and Lavena have their stand, is the older part of the square, and in the sixteenth century when Scamozzi designed and later Longhena finished the Procuratie Nuove on the opposite side, they made certain of greater safety and sloped the square to raise the arcade several steps.

In front of Florian's a throng watches in the uncertain light. Even there bubbling water seeps from a slit in the pavement, an unsuspected and unnoticed drain, and the trickle of water pools in an ever-widening circle.

The water has isolated San Marco and is kept only by the high door lintels from entering in cascade into the atrium below. Spread out before it is a fantastic vision of lacy tracery, dark arches and domes reflected in the moonlit waters of a tranquil night. The water has long since passed the columns of San Marco and San Todaro on the Piazzetta and breaks in little waves more than halfway to the Campanile's base. The columns of the Ducal Palace rise from lapping water.

But the turn of the tide has come and slowly the waters and the throng disperse.

In winter, occasionally, the tides rise much higher and water invades the Piazza to such an extent that gondolas can pass into the center of the square itself, but woe unto the unwary gondolier who is caught there with his gondola. A gondola *in piazza* would be a *contravvenzione* of a serious sort. It is perhaps this instinctive fear of being grounded on dry land which explains their avoidance, too, of the shallows of the lagoon. To be trapped there would be a real confession of impotence to the gondolier.

From the Piazzetta sounds the deep-voiced *Gondola, Gondola* of the gondoliers' calling, the deep toned "o" of the accented first syllable sounding almost like a "u," the accent giving a kind of instinctive motion to the word as if it, too, responds to the pulsing stroke of the oar.

Venice seems to gather to herself the undulant movement of the gondola, the movement of the lagoon, the movement of the waters of her canals; stepping from the gondola, Piazzetta, Piazza, all seem to sway with the same persuasive rhythm. At such a time the imagery of Shakespeare's words seems not too improbable:

> The cloud-capp'd towers, the gorgeous palaces,
> The solemn temples, the great globe itself,
> Yea, all which it inherit, shall dissolve;
> And, like this insubstantial pageant faded,
> Leave not a rack behind. We are of such stuff
> As dreams are made on, and our little life
> Is rounded with a sleep.
>
> *(The Tempest)*

"Such stuff as dreams are made on," of such is Venice.

iii

LE DUE VENEZIE

Two nets, symbolic of the sea, are cast with seeming carelessness upon the islands which cluster in the broad lagoon to form Venice—two nets cast abstractly, set one upon another, upon an established pattern. But they have no real relation to each other, only a functional relationship to the land they surround or serve.

The islands large and small which form the basic pattern were originally sandbars fringed by reeds. What their numbers were or are is hard to say, perhaps a hundred or so. Yet solid or solidified by the hand of man, they eventually achieved their present form, as the piles upon which the buildings rest were driven into the yielding sand. Stones, matting, the deposit of century upon century of life, the pavements each in turn, or together, gave the precarious solidity which Venice has. While human hand may have shaped these islands in part, fringing them with palace, church, or simple house, the exigencies of life have brought change as well. Canals which were superfluous disappeared and became land to leave only a memory and a name. Rio Terrà Antonio Foscarin, Rio Terrà dei Nomboli, or some such other, show where these canals were originally. Also the *Piscine,* small lakes formed by the rainwaters, were filled in to become Piscina Sant'Agnese, Piscina del Forner. Yet while this changing of the original pattern has long since ceased, the *Rio Terrà,* the filled canal, and the *Piscina,* the filled pond, still play their part in the nomenclature of Venice.

But the primary net which binds Venice together is the combination of canal and *rio,* the large and the small; it is an abstract pattern of water, yes, but like so many abstractions, expressive of an inner purpose. For it is these moving waters which are the principal means of communication, as they are the waterways along which move the heavy merchandise, the ways and byways of water transport.

The Grand Canal, the Canal of the Giudecca and that of Canareggio are the only waterways properly called canals, although the term is formally used as well for certain of the larger waterways which thread the lagoon. Each of the others is technically a *rio*—Rio San Trovaso, Rio San Moisè, Rio San Vio. Yet canal or *rio*, they fall under the generic name "canal" and are usually referred to in the aggregate under that name.

Upon this complex of land and water another net has been imposed, spun this time by the hand of man. This spiderweb of footways, in their origin, largely adventitious, runs everywhere throughout Venice, threading its way over more than four hundred bridges to give the ease of communication which a great city needs. Broad *fondamenta* line the Bacino di San Marco, the Giudecca Canal and to the east the Fondamenta Nuova, which faces the island of San Michele. Other larger arteries are called *ruvo*, to be translated *rue* or street. Famous is the Ruvo degli Orifici by the Rialto, lined with houses and shops, originally the street of the jewelers. Further, the *salizzada* are the streets first laid out, the *ramo* being the short connecting links between main thoroughfares. But it is these footways and the innumerable *calle*, that intricate complication of alleys large and small, which join together Piazza, Piazzetta, *campi, campielli,* and *corti,* areas which in descending scale form the open spaces and courtyards which dot Venice. These in their turn are the centers around which the community life of the various *sestieri,* or wards, revolves.

To one who knows only the Venice of the canals or the *rii,* the *calli* are a complete mystery. Each *calle,* or for that matter, each *rio,* winds in an unordained manner here and there, and each pattern is completely different. They haven't the least relationship to each other; they merely touch and mesh as the bridges cross. Venice would be a zero if it were judged by the cold generalizations of the city planner. Here the unexpected and the unplanned are the usual.

The Grand Canal, the Canal of the Giudecca, and a few of the others excepted, the pattern of the smaller canals, the *rii,* is an indescribable one. One leaves orientation aside and places one's trust implicitly in the gondolier, who perforce knows his city with exactness and can thread his way through *rii* large and small to his goal. Certainly no crow ever flew the way he goes. The gondolier may estimate distance as it is affected by known traffic or expected traffic, or perhaps by the tide—whether it is *in favore* or not. But he knows infallibly the shortest water route between two points. Anyone who follows a course on a map from San Marco to Sacca della Misericordia, for example, can understand its logic; however without a map the course taken is completely incomprehensible, cutting the broad reverse curve of the Grand Canal, weaving in and out of that canal as it does, one, two, and three times.

LE DUE VENEZIE

The ways of the land seem easier at first thought, for water is impersonal and leaves no lasting track. On land, if the thread of traffic is noticed, one can come out somewhere. It may not be the exact place sought—it may very likely be something you were looking for another time and did not find—but if you follow, at least it will not lead into an impasse or, worse still, to the dead end of a canal. But if there is no traffic and you choose to follow your own sense of direction and to find your way through instinct, only God can be your help. You will probably end in a cul-de-sac or, failing that, find yourself debouching into the Piazza di San Marco which you had just left a few moments before; you had intended to reach the Rialto instead. Knowledge and familiarity are the essentials, and these come only with time. But who has not had his orientation completely confounded and been suddenly confronted with the Campanile or the tower of the Frari appearing over buildings in a wrong direction and in a completely illogical place? One must learn that the broad path may not be the right one and a narrow alley may be the main stream. And there is another trick: the path of many feet, finding endlessly the same track, wears down pavements. That can be an aid if you are as clever as the American Indian in following man's footsteps.

These are the *Due Venezie,* the two Venices: the Venice of the canals and the Venice of the footways. They are equally rewarding, but each must be painstakingly learned by itself; then they can be related and through knowledge brought together. For upon the abstract pattern of nature lies the abstract pattern cast by the life of man.

25

The Dogana, Francesco Guardi, oil. Poldi-Pezzoli Museum, Milan.

iv

FULL MOON

It was full moon. The basin of San Marco was alive with gondolas; the *serenata,* the boats filled with musicians, were surrounded, the voices of the singers shriller and more stentorian than ever. At the head of the Grand Canal, above the point of the Dogana, the dome of Santa Maria della Salute dominated everything in the moonlight. How Longhena had sensed and expressed there the baroque soul of seventeenth-century Venice, in the dome with great scrolls which so proudly buttress it; and the broad steps which lead from three forward sides in cascaded flight to the water's edge. It is the sumptuous Venice of the Grand Canal.

But there is another Venice, the other side of the page, indivisible from the other—but so few turn the page. One has only to slip to the left past the arcaded point of the Dogana, housed in the slim, elongated triangle stretching in point of exclamation into the basin of San Marco. About it the tides whirl with greater force than in any other place in Venice. A gondolier at times can hardly make headway against them. At night to one side is the gaiety and brightness of the Grand Canal, to the other, the silent stretches of the Giudecca Canal.

However, there is animation enough there during the day with the movement of the tramps seeking the port of Venezia-Mestre on the terra firma or tying up at the Marittima. Often passenger ships pass on their way to unload their caravans—Americans, British, Italian, or travelers from the Near or Far East. There is excitement in it, for has not the sea always been mindful of

FULL MOON

Venice? It has brought her wealth and splendor through the centuries, and the life-blood of commerce flows again through her veins. When the unthinking long only for the picturesque past, secure in the possession of *confort moderne*, let them not forget that while Venice is in a sense a national monument, the tides of life still play unceasingly about her shores and make her real. She is no Mont St. Michel, no Aiguesmortes, no Carcassonne.

Here hidden behind the Dogana—so close at hand, only a stone's throw from the Grand Canal—is a night world unknown to most foreigners, perhaps only unconsciously felt by the Venetian himself who chances to pass by. After the brilliance of the Piazza, there was this silent wonder-world of ships lying quietly there, tucked behind the Salute. However, the ships do not lie there as once they did, for the exigencies of politics, war, and nationalism have broken many age-long ties between Venice and Dalmatia.

Then the *traboccoli* lay clustered along the Fondamenta della Zattere, or moored a few spans away with high-piled loads of firewood to be bargained for—*traboccoli* from Istria and Dalmatia, clustering there as they had in the time of the republic when the Adriatic was a Venetian lake. Time had left them and their function untouched until the war years, those strange, blunt-nosed ships with tangle of cordage, with pungent wood odors of their remembered highlands, with curious eyes banded in scarlet and azure and green painted upon their bows, with names upon the sterns enclosed in elaborate cartouches, bringing a quick vision of their homeland. And, just as surely, the man who then watched the simmering pot beneath a tiny awning at the stern or performed some other homely task, or he who rested in the cool of the evening was but a link in the long line of those who had gone to sea to find instinctively their market place in this tiny corner of the lagoons. Alas, what can it be that they have found to replace their humdrum tasks in what must be days of bitter reorientation?

But even memory, even the nightly passing of a spot cannot quite prepare for a night of full moon. Over the corner of the Seminario there is a flash of radiance, and the movement of the gondola slackens to glide noiselessly below the lowering shadow of a bark. Suddenly the curtain parts—a high wall, dark cypress trees cut sharply a vision of silver, of domes and towers. Is this Venice or Samarkand? No, it is truly Venice, it is the Salute, a temple built by Venetians to the glory of the Madonna, a thank-offering for the deliverance from the plague.

But there had been a meed of truth in the instinctive thought of Samarkand, for the East is always deeply felt in Venice. The dome had traveled from far Iran to the shores of the Bosporus, to be glorified in the Basilica of Hagia Sophia, in Santi Apostoli and other churches. And the Venetians, avid always for the beauties of the Near and Far East, had transplanted the idea again. On the muck of the lagoon they had built a great church in honor of their patron, the Evangelist Mark; it is a treasure house of domes and pinnacles, wrought of mosaic and porphyry, of brick and onyx and many a variegated marble brought from the four quarters of the globe. In its essence, the Basilica of San Marco is Byzantine, basically touched and altered by Venetian ideas and influences. Then, some six centuries later, another great church is built, the Salute, now purely Venetian. Yet in the very use of the dome there is a haunting remembrance of the Venetian past, of San Marco, and a nostalgia for those dreamed-of lands whose rich treasures had been transported across the sea in many a Venetian argosy.

The dome upon its octagon faces on Canalazzo, but here from the Zattere the smaller dome of the choir hides behind and builds to the central mass, flanked by the two bell towers which have the thrust of minarets. The somber depths of the shadows and the dark trees force the feeling of unreality, while above them the domes hover in their iridescence and their radiance.

The gondola rides on a sea of light. A dog barks. The water ripples against the black hulls. There is only the gentle splash and drip of the water from the oar.

v

CAMPI AND CANALS

The Piazza di San Marco alone is honored by the title *Piazza,* and there is, needless to say, only one Piazzetta, that continuation of the major space which leads to the water's edge, framed by the wonder of Sansovino's Library and the arcaded glories of the Ducal Palace. The Piazzetta dei Leoni is given that name only by courtesy. All the other open spaces in Venice, and there are many, are called *campi*—Campo Santo Stefano, Campo Sant' Angelo, Campo Santa Marguerita, Campo San Giacomo dell'Orio. What a host of pictures these names call up, each with its own particular character, each *populare,* of the people, not courtly, *signorile,* like the Piazza di San Marco, with that peculiar and lovable courtliness, *signorilità,* which allows a place for every class of the population—*signore, borghese, popolo.* Few foreigners come to know well these little open places tucked away amid the teeming life of a great city, there for the seeking but not always easy to find.

Far distant from the life of the Piazza is the Campo San Giacomo dell'Orio, a half circle of open space around the church of that name. Recent years have planted it with trees and today it is a place of shade around three *pozzi,* well curbs which served the needs of more primitive generations. Behind the wall of the church peeped for a time a pine planted there by a lover of the beautiful. It was planned to frame the church twenty, thirty, forty years and more from now, and hang over its enclosing wall. But for an unfeeling axe, Venice would have had one more thing to be grateful for because an artist cared for his adopted city and, more Venetian than the Venetians, gave his life to serve her.

31

At one end the Trattoria alla Vida closes the simple square. Before it a pergola of grapevines shields the front; the tables push out into the square, edged by tubbed plants. The sign over the door, *Alla Vida,* the Venetian for *Alla Vita,* "at the Sign of the Grapevine," gives its peculiar local flavor to a name from which even the baldness of translation cannot remove the charm.

Green of vines, grey of stone pavement, deep blue of an evening sky from which the light has not yet passed, pearl grey of stone and marble, red-washed walls, white tablecloths, the yellow wine, *Soave,* good friends, all compose the picture for an evening meal in which scampi fritti play no insignificant part.

Fringe of vines thrown into an intricate pattern of greens by the lantern light, fringe of vines against a sky now dark, throws into perspective the profile of San Giacomo dell'Orio, church of beautiful name, its walls touched by the light of dim street lamps. Around it is the open space of trees, and beneath them the curving side of the Campo circles and disappears beyond the three Romanesque apses of the church. On the farther side the stark, bald, powerful Campanile springs slimly from the pavement of the square to the Romanesque arcading of the *cella campanaria* and its pointed top. Proudly and simply the bells ring from this belfry, filling the square below with their melody. It is a square full of the sound of living, a Venice of Venetians, far from the cosmopolitan world.

From all this movement and animation the gondola slips quietly into the peace of the canals. The irregular roof lines frame a strip of star-filled sky. "Nocturne: Palaces" rise from the waters in which they repeat themselves in shimmering reflection, full of long lines, verticals, accented by the *pali* which mark palace doors. Whistler with a kind of divination realized this particular aspect of Venice as no one else has ever done. Even the most hardened believer in modernism and three-dimensional space cannot gainsay this shadowy existence, even if as subject matter he might pass it by. There this dream world is and Whistler caught it in its insubstantiality, a stage setting for all the unreality of a Venetian night.

At other times the canals have a strangely abstract quality. Perhaps it is the evening of the *Tombola*, a glorified bingo in the Piazza di San Marco which has brought untold thousands into that great meeting place of all Venice. The *festa* is finished; the *calli* leading from the Piazza fill with people, a solid stream of humanity. The gondola waits in the Bacino Orseolo and in a moment it slips into the anonymity of the little canals. Only the lighted bridges and the streaming thousands, diluted now by multitudinous byways, punctuate the quiet and relate one to the crowd of which one has been a part such a little time before. It is the transverse movement as if the woof of animation had suddenly been thrown across the silent warp of the canals.

Nocturne: Palaces, James McNeill Whistler, etching and drypoint. The Cleveland Museum of Art, Leonard C. Hanna Jr. Collection.

vi

WHITE NIGHTS

There is no quiet like the quiet of Venice when quiet falls. Never is there the sustained roar of a great city which does not sleep. The walls, so resonant at times, give no answering echoes. The *calli* are silent; the stones give back the vagrant footstep and are silent too. But there is an individuality always in every sound, whatever it may be; it is never sound merged with sound.

Constants there are, but of another kind—the lapping of water, the rush of wavelets as they run along the *fondamenta* wall—persuasive sounds that never cease. There is a brilliant life, a vitality which imposes itself when the winds are high. Then sound is rife and every other sound is stilled beneath the rhythmic battering of the sea. The water slaps and sparkles, splashes and throws up its spume of spray. It is like something charged. It hisses, sends aloft its effervescence, its champagne bubbles. The wind drops and there is only the relaxed reiteration of the waves, the sound of water as it washes up and down eternally.

This is not the reason the Venetian sleeps with shutters closed. The shutters insulate him against the noises of the passerby, against the *zanzari*, mosquitoes, and the flies. They shut out the light, too, when morning comes, and a modicum of air meanwhile slips in quite unobserved. It may be that they also give assurance against the thief who climbs and sees temptation in open windows close at hand.

When Venice sleeps, it sleeps. The bells are stilled; even the voices on the *fondamenta* are no more. But for a moment there is song, a gondolier passes by and along the far canal there is the distant silver of his voice, the voice beneath the window, then the trailing away of that melody as he passes across the broad canal to the Giudecca and his home. That gondolier, alas, does not sing as once he did. Then a moment of wakefulness was treasured, and if sleep did not return at once, the memory of those notes merged always with the rhythmic movement of the waves.

Utter silence. There is a distant voice; it disappears. Silence again. A sudden staccato of voices rise in sharp altercation; they fade. The softness of the Venetian dialect shades into the night. There is a deeper silence than before. A cat creeps. Another crawls, crouches, and pounces upon some denizen of the night. They creep away without a sound. Suddenly there is a caterwauling which seems in the silence to reach the summit of pure sound. It too passes and again night closes in.

Truly, at night Venice is the Venice of the past. There is no steady pulse of motors. They are silent, too, and for a moment the modern world is shut away, forgotten. It is the Venice of a thousand years, the city that was built upon Rialto's shores.

There is no early chatter of the birds. The pigeons of the Gesuati roost in their familiar places, accenting Massari's architecture with changing darks, but they are far away. Their gentle sound cannot be heard. The faint light of morning touches a distant wall. The skies lighten. The bells of the Gesuati begin their silver chant.

MY GARDEN IS BEYOND THE WALL

My garden is beyond the wall. From my windowed balcony one sees obliquely a wall of crumbling brick weathered by long years of wind and weather. Time has touched this wall with kind hands; its red bricks have softened to salmon and to rose, darkened above the grey-white Istrian stone, where the dust of *fondamenta* has risen and adhered. Where hands could touch, the vagrant hand has left a patina, edges of single bricks have gently softened, mortar between them falling away to leave an accent and a warmer tone. Moisture has crept down, veiling the bricks with a voile of greyish white. Vines hang almost to obscure painted letters on an oblong targe: *Fondamenta Bragadin.*

The corner slides away to meet a concave bay. The wall graciously retires to let *fondamenta* meet *fondamenta* and free traffic from the Ponte della Calcina, where Rio San Vio and the Canal of the Giudecca meet. Brick piers receive the gentle curve of this bay. A cupid looks across the broad waters from the nearer corner. Is it in protest that he holds away from him an open book so that only those who cross the bridge can read? A brother *putto*, nearly hidden beneath the foliage of laurels, peers towards the canal. Tendrils climb around him as he shrinks into the shadow to seek refuge there.

My garden is beyond the wall, a space of quiet and of peace. The world passes by outside its walls, footsteps muffled and voices stilled. I see a single cypress at the farther end, the clear, staccato line which punctuates a palace wall. The silver leaves of the olive flash in brilliant contrast to the somber darks above—sixteenth notes that throw into relief the major theme. The sharp greens of the pines sway and their spiny joints seem staid and stiff beside the frivolous movement of the olive branches as the wind tosses them, twinkling, here and there.

And many are the trees and plants which grace my garden—*lecce,* laurel, *edera,* oleander. The wax-like leaves of the latter shine, highlighted by the deep rose and white of its flowers. There is the sharp and acid yellow-green of wisteria, the flower long since past. Near at hand a poplar, transparent, moves gay and free. The erect column of its form opens, closes. The leaves turn and glitter in the sun as the wind brushes them—vermeil in contrast to the silver olive trees. Extrovert and introvert, poplar and cypress provide the scale the long, low palace needs. A file of grey-green shutters seen in sharp perspective marches along the front façade. An iron balcony, balustered, wraps around the smaller end pavilion at the nearer end, wraps around to catch what vagrant winds there are.

When there is no sun, how rich and variegated is the palette of nature! The greyness of the sky brings out tones that vanish in the greater monotony of sunlight. Everything is golden then, the nostalgia of the minor mood has passed. It is now positive, direct, warm—the major mode. But when the moon shines, the trees go dark, the *putti* come out and dominate my wall, the palace looms, shivering slightly among the shadows, and a silver carpet is rolled before the palace door.

MY GARDEN IS BEYOND THE WALL

Gardens of Venice, hidden as my garden is beyond the wall, give their perfumes behind majestic palaces, or behind the simple homes where space is left for them, places of quietness within the network of the canals. In another mood they line the far Giudecca shore, small remnant of the rich orchards and gardens that once were there. Their cypresses, their oleanders, their olive trees look to the distant *lidi* across the broad lagoon, the sea lapping eternally against their boundary walls.

viii

FOR RENT

The house was tightly closed. The wooden shutters gave a sense of absolute finality, and if that was not enough, there was tacked on each shutter a rectangle of cardboard, a sign in Venice that a house is available for rent. On the second story the balcony looked into my garden beyond the wall. The long, unequal fronds of American ivy, *uva del Canada* as it is called in Italy, hung dripping along the entire front, green icicles which somehow congealed the heart even after these many years. Memories can warm, but here was tragedy and emptiness. The shutters had truly closed upon the past.

It was a late summer day in the twenties or the early thirties. The Signora had died. The heirs, friends, were there to clear the inheritance. It was the first time I had ever been in the house and it was sad enough, for the vitalizing presence had truly gone. I had never seen her. She was never seen in those last years. If she was on the balcony, a *tenda*, an awning, hung. One knew there was a presence there, but that was all. One never caught a glimpse of her. She was old and tired, lived only in her past. The windows of the house were open then, of course, but they seemed to open in, not out.

She was one of the minor personalities of Venice of whom one spoke. The older people had known her and once in a while in those days some member of that generation slipped within the doors, but those became ever fewer as death took its toll.

The house itself had rare personality and charm. It was filled with things which in a past century could still be bought—fine chairs with ribbon backs, with that peculiar and gracious style which eighteenth century Venice always had. The long sofas and settees craved the cushions that were there to make them comfortable. A lacquer cabinet was a most lovely and precious thing, but later it seemed strange and out of place in Kent, Ohio. It was yellow, a yellow touched with green, slightly acid, a color which approached the chartreuse of a later age when Dorothy Draper dominated a decorative world. Here was reticence, refinement. Slant-eyed mandarins promenaded slowly beneath umbrellas of silk, or sat beneath fanciful pagodas and dreamed strange dreams, read poetry, or painted with the fluid brush-stroke of the Far East. But this was Venetian, too, with that interpretation which the Venetian always gave to what was hers. Venice had touched the Orient in the time of Marco Polo and that memory still lived. *Chinoiserie,* the Chinese mode, had become the fashion in a Europe which always sought the beauties of the distant and unknown.

There were Venetian boxes of lacquer, too, that could be locked. One was yellow with a gracious, curving shape, slightly bellied as if a breeze had filled its sails. *Gonfio* is the Italian word; in English, "blown up" is banality itself. But there was no banality here. Flowers in little nosegays sprinkled the surface and gave a note of frivolity and gaiety. Another finely profiled box, rectangular in shape, of a strange, acid green looked to the Orient as well, a more serious and retrospective East, contemplative and mysterious, too. It was capacious and it also locked with a key.

But the boxes were empty now. The personal things had somehow disappeared. What was left was the mere framework of a life, which did not explain what that life had really been.

She had been beautiful, desirable, lovely in a reticent, English way, with a complexion and coloring which in Venice always brought remark and the admiring glance. It was the period when a complexion of rose and white was something to conjure with. All women were not reduced to the dull monotony, to the "bronzed livery of the sun."

She had been loved and courted by an Englishman of high birth, a *Milord,* as the Italians says so charmingly. She had been gay with the gaiety which comes from happiness. But there was a question of inheritance, some curious impediment which meant he could not marry until the problem was resolved. Letters passed back and forth for years, it seemed—letters of love, devotion, everlasting loyalty, no doubt. She tied them in little packets of ten, each with a ribbon, and placed them in her *scatole* of lacquer, her lacquer boxes, and closed them with a key.

There were delirious moments when he came to Venice. They floated on enchanted waters in the cool evenings of the hot days of summer. She lived for those days and for those letters which always came. There was a hint of sadness, though, in her eyes in the winter days when she was alone. Time passed—years, in fact, and the problem never seemed to be resolved. The first freshness of her beauty passed, but to it was added a new loveliness which came with the years.

Then suddenly the letters stopped. One never knew the reason why. Her life stopped, too. The doors which had been always open, closed, except for the very few who were admitted to her intimacy. She lived the life of a recluse with her memories, her letters. She always carried the key, the key which unlocked her lost world, about her neck, suspended on a long chain of gold which disappeared within the mysteries of her dress.

It was a period in the last decade of the nineteenth century when Venice was truly gay. Henry James lived for a time in the Palazzo Barbaro on the Grand Canal with the Curtisses of Boston and wrote some of his finest work in that incomparable framework. Milly Teale is sketched against the background of a Venice of which he had divined the soul. It is never a banal account of the outer Venice, no mere recounting of her monuments. It is the intimate life of a city which dreams dreams and where, perchance, dreams come true. Or do they disappear in the *caligo,* the *nebbia,* the fog which comes in early morning in the autumn days?

Could James have known the early part of this story of the lady? One cannot say. That he did know of something similar one can be certain, for in the *Aspern Papers,* published in 1888, he writes a short novel which had details not dissimilar.

The years passed. The lady who had looked for so long into the garden that was beyond the wall was old indeed. She had lived there for one never knew how many years, more than fifty, I believe. She was a legend in herself, a legend which grew with the telling. But those who knew the legend died and there was silence, too. The letters were now fragile, yellowed. The ink faded gradually with the years.

She died. Her will outlined in complete detail what should be done with what she had. And first of all, the letters were to be burned unread. The British Consul performed his duty well, but he had to do that which the law prescribed. He had to read each letter before it was destroyed. But no word of what he read was ever known.

A burst of flame, a puff of smoke, a heap of ashes lay upon the hearth. A trace of smoke hovered about the chimney pot and then was dissipated above the Venice she had loved so well. The shutters closed upon the past, and tacked on each one of them was the telltale rectangle. The house is still for rent.

ix

FRESCO IN CANALAZZO

Fresco in Canalazzo was originally the designation for a social custom which could only grace an earlier time when elegance and social rule were sacrosanct, determined as they were by laws as fixed as the laws of the Medes and the Persians. Zanetti, in his *Memorie,* defines the term, *Fresco, Passeggiata in gondola scoperta in Canal Grande,* which may be roughly translated "a turn in the Grand Canal in an open gondola." Here the added term *Canalazzo*—the termination—*azzo* added to *canal*—expresses effectively under this appellation the rather special character of the Grand Canal, the main artery of Venice.

The *Fresco in Canalazzo* originates as early as the seventeenth century, when even the time and the dates became fixed, the *Fresco* beginning the second Sunday after Easter and continuing on the Sundays and the feast days until the end of September. As a custom it fell into gradual disuse until it was taken up again with renewed enthusiasm in the second half of the eighteenth century, continuing to be the mode as late as the time of Lord Byron in the nineteenth century. One can imagine the handsome and romantic English *Milord,* poet and dreamer, gracing the gondola of one of the great beauties of the moment, the cynosure of all eyes, desired by many.

Could any other vehicle be more adapted to show off the perfections of a beautiful woman than a gondola—if a gondola can be called a vehicle? Could any frame be more brilliant or rewarding than the Grand Canal? The great figures of Venice took their *Fresco* with their gondolas, their gondoliers in the picturesque liveries of the time. It was gracious and leisurely and *signorile,*

45

truly worthy of a gentleman or a great lady. The gondolas passed up and down the Canal, the occupants greeting their friends, ignoring their enemies. A bow from a great personage could make or break a day for those whose position in the social framework was insecure.

The custom was just as fixed in its rules as was the drive in Hyde Park for the London world in a later period. There the world of society took the air in their landaus, their coachmen and their footmen perfectly turned out, impeccable. They made their prescribed rounds, too, always with the hope of a bow from a certain royal personage, and they parceled out their greetings to their friends with as great care as did the ladies in Venice. Paris with its Bois de Boulogne, London with its Hyde Park, Venice with its *Fresco in Canalazzo*—what pictures these are of times and elegancies which are past. No more effective settings could be found for the display of which so much of life was made.

But the *Fresco in Canalazzo* in its original form died with its times; it could never exist in a democratic world. However, the idea lived, and with an application which is quite different. Basically, there still was the same desire of the Venetian to enjoy the coolness of the evening and to seek a few hours of pleasure and enjoyment after the heat of the day. So, once a summer, a night is chosen—whenever it may be, on any date which suits the fancy, for there was, as one can see, no historical significance, no historical implication whatsoever connected with the *Fresco in Canalazzo*. It is now a *festa* of all the people of

Venice, who with their visitors can relax and enjoy themselves together in the incomparable framework of the Grand Canal.

There are, to be sure, certain precautions which must be taken by the authorities, and blessedly, with them Venice becomes again the Venice of long ago. No motorboats are allowed on the Grand Canal. The *Vaporetto* is stopped for a given period, and if there are larger embarkations, they are permitted only when they are moored to the *fondamenta* or palace wall. In very truth, the gondola is king for a night.

There are many embarkations of many kinds which line the Grand Canal on that evening, each filled with eager viewers, families and friends crowded together to take up every available inch of space. Improvised stands are set up on some of the larger boats, such as the *peate*, and seats are sold. The *fondamenta* are filled to suffocation. Every available standing or, for that matter, sitting space, no matter how tiny, which gives access to the Grand Canal has its quota. The palace balconies and windows each have their eager spectators.

Venice is *en fête*. The floodlights illuminate with a happy reticence, binding the whole into festive pattern. The gondolas, their lanterns lit, dance upon the shimmering reflections of the Canal. The windows of the palaces are thrown wide. Their crystal chandeliers illuminate their thousand prisms and throw sparkling lights upon walls of crimson damask, upon portraits of ancestors who often must have looked down on scenes not so different from this. Painted and frescoed ceilings, rich decorations of stucco give an echo of the wonders of a past which still lives on.

But the focus, the center around which this all revolves is the *Galleggiante,* a latticed dome thrown over orchestra and singers to weave a spell of light and melody, multicolored lights which sparkle in the radiance of an evening of full moon.

> In Xanadu did Kubla Khan
> A stately pleasure dome decree
> Where Alph the sacred river ran
> Through caverns measureless to man
> Down to the sunless sea.
>
> ("Kubla Khan," Coleridge)

It is as simple as that, so simple—a command, a float, lights, and a dream is born.

The *Galleggiante* appears, moving slowly around the curve of the Grand Canal by San Geremia. Gondolas cluster in ever increasing numbers. The canal is paved with them. The *Galleggiante* stops. Utter silence! And in the perfect acoustics of this natural auditorium framed by palaces, the voices rise with perfect clarity and an enchanting beauty. Where but in Italy could you get such concentration? Where but in Italy could you bring together such a *publicum?* Every class, every age, every condition of life, even the most disparate are united for a moment, held spellbound by the perfection of a melody.

The last note of the orchestra ceases. The fireboat spouts its streams of water carefully and with such efficacy that the *Galleggiante* can find a path. All the gondoliers are on their feet. The canal resounds with the *Voga! Voga! Voga!* of the *Vigili*, the police, as they cry "Row! Row! Row!" Rythmically the great cortege flows. The bodies of the gondoliers are woven together in repeated movement. Each strives to ease his way ahead, to avoid his neighbor, calling to him in good natured bonhomie. Theirs is a fluidity which belongs to no other form of locomotion, a rhythmic excitement from the synchronization of so much effort. The mass of gondolas are as one and seem to glide on a path of glass.

The *Galleggiante* stops. There is silence. The gondoliers back water so as to come as close as possible to the music. The whole complex becomes an even more compact mass.

The excitement is at its height when the cortege comes close to the Rialto Bridge. Three or four hundred gondolas with the *Galleggiante*, spread over a broad canal, must be compressed into the smaller space. The music stops and the gondoliers race to pick their way. The *Voga! Voga! Voga!* of the *Vigili* sounds more staccato, repeatedly, endlessly, demandingly. *Voga!* "Row!" Somehow the gondolas manage to file through. The dome of the *Galleggiante* is lowered to allow it to pass under the Rialto Bridge.

The gondolas rearrange themselves in the ample framework between the Riva del Carbon and the Rio del Vin. Here are concentrated thousands upon thousands. The *fondamenta* groan with milling crowds. There is silence again and

The Grand Canal, Venice, Francesco Guardi, oil. The Art Institute of Chicago, Wirt D. Walker Fund.

then the music of Donizetti in the mad scene from *Lucia di Lammermuir*. How could one ever have thought it trivial? Never has it seemed so right. Never has it seemed so real. Never has coloratura been better adapted to such an audience and such a proscenium. The liquid notes float higher, higher, ever higher in the pure perfection of sound for sound alone. Breathless, the crowd hangs on every trill, on every roulade until the voice leaps into the void in the final perfection of the Italian *do di petto*, the high E. For a long moment there is silence as that note lingers disembodied in the enchanted air.

One could think only of another unforgettable evening in the early twenties. In Venice a whisper becomes public knowledge in no time. This time it became stentorian and hundreds of gondolas congregated below the balconies of the Grand Hotel. Nellie Melba came forth and even the *vaporetto* were still for her as she sang the "Jewel Song" from *Faust*. Then she made her last farewell to the Venice she loved and was never to see again in the nostalgic melody of "The Last Rose of Summer."

But memories last and new memories are made this very night. This *Serenata*, this serenade of music, the *Galleggiante*, passes by San Samuele, by the Accademia to end the course before the steps of Santa Maria della Salute. *Fresco in Canalazzo!* The Venetians and their visitors have come together once more tonight to enjoy an evening of coolness on the Grand Canal.

x

THE PIAZZA DI SAN MARCO

The slanting rays of a late afternoon sun, filtered by clouds, gilded the mosaics and pinnacles of San Marco and warmed the soft apricot marbles of the walls of the Ducal Palace. Lavena's and Quadri's were full of their usual clientele, sipping their tea, drinking their beer or colored drink, orangeade, or the ancestor of Coca-Cola—in any case, the soft drink then in fashion. Others were more interested in their petty purchases, or in the mere satisfaction of the inner man.

There was an uncertainty in the sky, but it carried no hint of terror. As the sky darkened a bit, an anxious few paid their bills and sauntered beneath the arcades to window shop. A few drops of rain and the unhurried exodus accelerated. More rain and the Piazza began to empty quickly. Frightening darkness closed in. Lights flashed on. People crowded into the open doors of San Marco. People began to run to find what refuge they could, their coats flying out behind them like the vestments of the terror-stricken monks who fled from the lion of St. Jerome in the painting of Carpaccio's in San Giorgio degli Schiavoni.

There was an ominous silence broken by a distant roar, a shrill whine of wind, lashing and blinding rain, and then a whirlwind of sound and movement —metal tables and chairs lifted in the air, tossed aloft, caught and whirled, crashing together like gigantic cymbals in a witches' dance of overwhelming abandon. The metallic clangor of the storefronts closing meant nothing in this inferno of sound. The three great flags before the Basilica were in an instant torn to ribbons. The flagpoles twisted like matchsticks, disintegrated into a thousand pieces.

The tornado, for that it was, ended as quickly as it had begun. The waves which had swept over the *fondamenta*, sending the water far into the Piazzetta, gradually subsided. But in the Piazza the tables and the chairs were piled in masses here and there as if tossed aside by the force of a mighty torrent, inextricably mixed with the miserable detritus of destruction. Awnings fluttered in tattered shreds and everywhere lay hundreds of dead pigeons, dashed against the buildings or caught in the frightening whirlpool of chairs, tables, and other *impedimenti* which had risen almost as high as the roofs of the Procuratie.

There were no injuries in the Piazza itself, only minor contusions, as in the first moments waiters tried to bring a table or chair to safety. But there were two deaths—an elderly lady and her gondolier who were caught in the open lagoon when they imprudently set out for a nearby island. They were swept to their deaths despite the heroic efforts of the gondolier to bring his *padrona* to safety.

The Piazza has seen many events—cataclysms of nature such as this tornado, as well as many thrilling pages in the long chapters of history. Upon the square of red Veronese marble in the atrium, just inside the main portal of San Marco, Pope Alexander III and the Holy Roman Emperor, Frederick Barbarossa, met in 1177, their quarrels ended. A High Mass in the Basilica

Piazza San Marco, Venice, Francesco Guardi, drawing. The Cleveland Museum of Art, John L. Severance Fund.

celebrated a new understanding between Pope, Emperor, and the Commune. It is probable that they later showed themselves to the people from the Loggia which surmounts the five portals. Here in 1364, Petrarch, as he records it in his *Letters*, assisted at a tourney in honor of the great victory of Candia.

The four Greek horses from the Hippodrome in Constantinople look across the Piazza today as they have for centuries. The only original mosaic of the façade, that over the left doorway, dating from about 1270-1280, records them graphically as being then in place. They had been placed there by the Venetians as a symbol of their spectacular victory in 1204, part of the immense booty taken from Constantinople in the brutal sack by the crusading army. Venice has often been bitterly judged for this, but the Venetian could not forget the treachery of the Emperor Manuel and the pitiless killing of ten thousand of her citizens in Constantinople some thirty-three years before; in the course of history, one cruel deed has too often bred another.

But was it with a purpose that the Venetians placed the horses as they are, so that the heads of the outside horses turn inward, instead of outward as they once did in the Quadriga in Constantinople? Did they reverse that outer pair with the intent that they would not think of other horizons, but would hold their gaze always within the confines of the Piazza? Certainly it was only the compelling urgencies of a World War which could have let them out for a while to graze in the green security of a Roman *cortile*—an appropriate *cortile*, at that, for it was the central court of the Palazzo Venezia in Rome. Once before, they

A Procession of Triumphal Cars in Piazza S. Marco, Venice, Francesco Guardi, drawing.
The Cleveland Museum of Art, John L. Severance Fund.

had deserted Venice, willy-nilly, when the imperial greediness of Napoleon made him dream of placing them on the summit of the Arc du Carrousel in Paris. But his dream was never realized, and it was not long before the horses returned to familiar scenes.

Great processions used to wind around the Piazza as a matter of course, and a great painter, Gentile Bellini, has left an unforgettable pictorial representation of such an event on the canvas painted for the Scuola Grande di Giovanni Evangelista, now in the Accademia. In a more fugitive fashion, Guardi recorded with his pen the fêtes given there in 1782 on the occasion of the visit of the Conti di Nord, the hereditary princes of Russia. Even today, if in much less splendor, a procession of the highest clergy wends its way across the Piazza each mid-July and then over the Grand Canal and the Giudecca on bridges of boats to the Redentore, Palladio's great church on the nearer Giudecca shore.

Great figures, or figures who have loomed high in the history of their time, have always been greeted here in the Piazza by the public. Yet it is a symbol of changed times and different loyalties that the political world has been quite separated from the spiritual, and that in decades not too long past, Hitler, Goebbels, Mussolini, and the King Emperor, appeared before the public not on the terrace of San Marco, but from the central balcony of the Royal Palace at the opposite end.

57

Venice: Piazza di San Marco and Piazzetta, Michiel Marieschi, etching. The Mr. and Mrs. Charles G. Prasse Collection.

The Campanile, isolated, faces on the right flank, opposite to and dominating the Basilica, guarding the junction of Piazzetta and Piazza. Its foundations are Romanesque and ninth-century, but it found its all-but-final form between the twelfth and fourteenth centuries, still lacking its pointed pinnacle. Jacopo di Barbari's engraving of Venice, in its first state, records the Campanile after the burning of the temporary top in 1498. In the second state of the print, dated 1500, another top has been added, but it was only after the earthquake of 1511 that the Campanile was completed in its ultimate form. Struck by lightning many times, shaken by earthquakes, the Campanile continued to dominate the Venetian skyline for many centuries and gave every indication that it would long continue that vigil.

But that was not to be. The simple desire for warmth sparked a thoughtless act on the part of a custodian. He removed bricks, they say, from the interior wall to give sufficient space for a fire and by his action brought unexpected and unnecessary strains on the fabric. Shortly afterwards slight cracks were noted on the exterior wall near this point. The cracks began to lengthen gradually, and what was worse, to widen. There was natural concern on the part of the authorities, but no real alarm. The Campanile had, after all, passed through many vicissitudes. Yet for security, ropes were placed somewhat futilely around the base and no one was allowed to ascend the spiral ramp which led to the top. The Venetian casually walked around to inspect and conjecture. But had not there been intimations of danger before and nothing come of them? The cracks began to widen. Still the *Banda Municipale* played as scheduled in the Piazza, crowded with the evening throng of listeners who in the intermission sauntered around to look. Suddenly the authorities, greatly concerned, as well they might be, abruptly stopped the concert, and the ropes were placed at a greater distance from the base. Yet the Venetian merely shrugged his shoulders and did not worry.

At ten o'clock the next morning, July 14, 1902, things went on as usual in the Piazza. There was the usual number of visitors feeding the pigeons, when with no further warning, the Campanile collapsed upon itself. The miracle is that it did what it did—for if it had fallen one way, it would have destroyed San Marco; if it had fallen another way, it would have caused irreparable damage to the Ducal Palace. What it actually did was merely to destroy one small angle of Sansovino's Library. The porphyry column—the *pietra del bando* from which laws and condemnations were proclaimed—which stands before the right-hand corner column of the Basilica's façade by a miracle contained and held back the spreading debris from pressing upon that column and thus saved the façade of San Marco from collapse. But what was truly astonishing was that no human life was lost, no one was even injured.

A gondolier, seated in his gondola near the far point of the island of San Giorgio Maggiore, sat half dozing as his *padrone* painted. That painter could never forget to his dying day the wild cry of the gondolier as he sprang to his feet, or the expression of unbelieving horror and emotion on his face. He had seen the Campanile disappear, and as the painter whirled to look there was nothing but a cloud of dust, gradually spreading, blotting out the Ducal Palace, the Basilica of San Marco, the Piazzetta itself. When the dust had settled, Venice had lost indeed the element towards which all her architecture aspired, the focus, the crowning feature, the symbol which the Venetians had so well understood as such when they built it in the days of their might.

The impact upon Venice can be imagined. A friend buying cigarettes in a shop near the Bocca di Piazza stood rooted to the ground, paralyzed with fear, as overwhelming sound filled the air, crowded upon him, and staggered his every sense. When he rushed out, the Piazza was filled with an impenetrable cloud of dust. For a moment there seemed to be no sound, then the clap-clap of running feet and the multitudinous flapping of the many thousand wings of pigeons wheeling in wild alarm. The dust settled and the entire Piazza was filled with thousands, their faces streaked with ruddy brick dust. All Venice wept, wept uncontrollably.

And well they might, for the Campanile in a very peculiar sense incorporated the pride of Venice in herself. Its pinnacle was the sailors' last vision of their homeland as her fleets sailed to make the eastern Mediterranean a Venetian lake. It was the last point on the far horizon as her mariners crossed the Adriatic to further seas, to seek and transport in their argosies the riches of the East and to pile upon her *fondamenta* the treasures which brought untold wealth to her merchants. The Campanile was the symbol of their city when the Venetian ships came back in their days of triumph, a point of light in the darkness, an exclamation mark profiling itself against the distant sky. And when, from the

Piazza di San Marco, Francesco Guardi, oil. The Virginia Museum of Fine Arts, Richmond.

arcade of its *cella campanaria* far above the city, eager watchers caught the first flash of their sails, their lights, all Venice reeled with the triumphant clangor of a thousand bells.

But in the face of such a tragedy there was no lack of decision. That very night in the great hall of the Ducal Palace, the *Consiglio Communale* met in solemn session, and it was decided with unanimous consent that the Campanile should be rebuilt: "Dov'era, Com'era"—"Where it was, as it was." As it was ordered so was it done; and on April 25, 1912, the new Campanile, "El papà dei campanile," was dedicated on the feast of San Marco, patron saint of Venice. So once more Venice had its Campanile, *El paron di casa*, the master of the house.

The very manner of its fall, however, had brought with it its own wonder. As the Venetians said in their soft dialect, *Se ca sentà come un zentilomo*; "it sat down like a gentleman," and in very truth, it did so, with a minimum of confusion, in utter simplicity. But more wonderful than all, what in the eyes of many was the culmination of the miracle, was that the *Marangona*, the largest of the five bells whose deep tones announced the working hours, and the Archangel Gabriel, the gilded *girouette* which from the very summit indicated the direction of the wind and which crowns the reconstructed Campanile today, rode the ruin in its fall, cushioned in some unimaginable way by the disintegrating fabric—both to rest finally upon the top of the spreading mass of rubble. And there the Archangel stood erect, his hand pointing triumphantly to the Basilica which he had so miraculously protected from destruction.

View of the Piazza San Marco, Venice, and the Piazzetta Looking towards San Giorgio Maggiore, Giovanni Antonio Canal (Canaletto), oil.
The Cleveland Museum of Art, purchase, Leonard C. Hanna Jr. Bequest.

xi

GEOMETRIC PATTERNS

The geometry of the Piazza di San Marco and the Piazzetta is quite out of the ordinary. Only on analyzing it carefully does one have any idea of their considerable irregularity. For the first impact is overwhelming. It is like a lovely woman who utterly enchants by her personality, by her beauty, her sparkling vivacity and character, her certain presence, her overwhelming charm. Only later, with reflection, is there surprise. Her features are not regular. They may not even be perfect in themselves. Yet life has been good. She has rare individuality and character, and character is one of the all-important elements which adds up to perfection.

Venice has character, and in no single spot does she weave the spell of enchantment more completely than in the Piazza and the Piazzetta. But even there, after many years of familiarity, Venice is still the enigma, the unexpected.

The actual form of the Piazza when first approaching through the arcades of the Bocca di Piazza, at the opposing end from San Marco, may seem at first glance to be rectangular or just slightly out of the rectangular. The Basilica is thrown into sharp perspective from here by the mass of the Campanile. The slight angling of the Procuratie Vecchie to the left gradually broadens the Piazza, almost imperceptibly at first, and gives air and a sense of space. For the Piazza, in its essence, is but the framework, exquisite in itself, almost like the creation of a goldsmith, whose purpose is to bring to full value the fantastic beauties of this great church. To the left the Piazzetta dei Leoncini flanks it, a *piazzetta* named for the ridiculous lions in red Veronese marble, forever ridden, polished to utmost beauty of material by the continual friction of youthful bodies and occasionally one of greater age. To the right beyond the Campanile is the real Piazzetta, always called simply that—the Piazzetta.

There is no cluttering anywhere. The Venetians have never permitted anything which would spoil the perfection of their open spaces, although the great Condottiere Colleoni, a general of the Venetian army, bequeathed and Venice accepted money for his equestrian statue by Verocchio to be placed in the Piazza di San Marco. But the Piazza was spared it when the statue was completed, for the *Signoria* quietly put the noble work where it is now, before the façade of SS. Giovanni e Paolo. Yet in the last century the authorities seem to have wavered a bit in their thinking. They went so far as to place between the columns of San Marco and San Todaro on the Piazzetta a plaster cast by a mediocre sculptor of Rome, Ettore Ferrari, his equestrian figure of Vittorio Emanuele II. But that was sufficient. Public opinion forced its immediate removal and the statue found its home, a more appropriate one, on the Riva degli Schiavoni where it could at least spoil no vistas.

The three great flagpoles in front of the Basilica are placed where they are with complete inevitability. One cannot imagine them anywhere else. Yet why is this so? They do not center on anything, though they seem to. What are they parallel to? Nothing. They are not parallel to the Napoleonic wing which now closes the farther end of the Piazza. They do not line up with the Loggetta of the Campanile but go off at a slightly different angle. They completely conflict with the line of the façade of San Marco. In fact, if both these lines were projected, they would meet near the column of San Todaro on the Piazzetta. Yet they are in this supremely effective position because someone with genius and feeling and judgment had the vision to place them there. Aesthetically they are magnificent, and it is a pity that they do not often carry out their real function. They should always fly their banners. This they do with much distinction only, alas, on days of great *festa*.

Sitting at one of the tables in the last file at Lavenas, San Marco seems almost incandescent with the sunset rays. They touch repeatedly the many Byzantine columns of the façade, outlining them with shadow, throwing darks beneath the arches, great and small, which range one behind another in sharpening perspective. The light caresses the curling Gothic cresting of the façade, the statues, the gilded pinnacles. Beyond, the sun falls on the diapered walls of the Ducal Palace. The Palace retires with reticence behind the corner of San Marco, but the columns and arches of the arcade which opens on the Piazzetta and the rich Gothic arcading of the loggias above are picked out with radiance. The column of San Marco is lined vertically. Sunlight divides it into half light, half dark shadow.

The Piazzetta also seems to be rectangular. In verity the rectangle of the Ducal Palace as a complex slants inward. The line of the Library, the *Biblioteca Marciana*, also converges. The line of the façade of San Marco, of the Loggetta of the Campanile, of the flagstaffs themselves, every line projects the eye

The Piazzetta, Francesco Guardi, oil. Ca' d'Oro, Venice.

through the twin columns of San Marco and San Todaro towards the stupendous climax of San Giorgio Maggiore.

The Piazza and the Piazzetta are thus a willed contrast, both a play of perspective. One with divergent lines holds the Basilica of San Marco like a jewel in its broad opening. The other builds its effect upon converging lines which lead through to a final perfection, Palladio's San Giorgio. San Marco opens its heart to you; the Piazzetta leads the eye to farther horizons.

Creations of the Byzantine, the Gothic, the Baroque—San Marco, the Ducal Palace, San Giorgio—move easily one behind the other, in sequence. It is a world of the spirit which the centuries have built. The light floods the Bacino di San Marco. It throws reflections on moving waters, on waves tipped with white in the brisk breeze of an autumn afternoon. One flank of the Campanile of San Giorgio catches the light. It is brilliant. One lies in shadow. The rosy tones of the brick of nave, transept, and conventual buildings are flushed with sunset. Against the colorful background the façade stands, simply, effectively. The fine Istrian stone with which it is built, *pietra d'Istria*, transported across the Adriatic in Venetian ships, has acquired a patina of ivory with the passing of the years. Truly, Palladio designed the façade of San Giorgio Maggiore to meet the setting of the sun.

San Giorgio Maggiore, Venice, Francesco Guardi, oil. The Toledo Museum of Art, gift of Edward Drummond Libbey.

xii

SAN GIORGIO MAGGIORE

The Island of San Giorgio was called from early times *Isola dei Cipressi,*
Isola Verde—the island of the cypresses, the green island. Closing the vista
from the Piazzetta and the Riva degli Sciavoni, as it does from many another
point, it lines the southern sky with its intricate pattern of trees, with the dome
and campanile of the great church dominating the complex of its structure and
the wonder of its Palladian façade. In earlier years the island was rich with
gardens and with vineyards. There were *saline*, salt beds to gather the salt of the
lagoons, a mill, a church dedicated to San Giorgio in the time of or before the
Participazio, a family which gave five doges to Venice in the ninth century.
However, it was the ceding of the island to Giovanni Morosini by Doge
Tribuno Memmi in 962 that founded a tradition which happily lives today. For
he built a Benedictine monastery there which was enriched by later gifts and
became a place of pilgrimage with the bringing of the body of San Stefano,
proto-martyr. Giovanni Morosini, as the first Abbot, started a tradition of study
which was to make the convent famous. In the fifteenth century even its
gardens became a place of *ritrovo* for the socratic disputes of Venetian noble
and scholar. For the Benedictine order has had for many centuries a continuing
record of devotion to and encouragement of intellectual pursuits and studies
in many fields.

At the time of the fall of the Republic in 1797, this tradition seemed to
have come to an end. Yet a Pope was elected here in Papal Conclave after the
death of Pope Pius VI, prisoner of Napoleon. The Conclave was held between
December, 1799, and March, 1800. The Venetians anxiously watched across the

waters of the Bacino for the tell-tale wisp of smoke, white or black, which
would tell whether the ballots of the Cardinals had brought results. Finally,
Cardinal Chiaramonte was elected Pope Pius VII. Then the monastery was
disestablished. Many of the splendid works of art which decorated it were
dispersed, among them the "Marriage of Cana," masterpiece of Paolo Veronese,
looted by Napoleon and taken to Paris where it is now one of the greatest
treasures of the Musée du Louvre. To be sure, the church was reopened to the
cult in 1807, but the time of greatness had departed, it seemed forever. In the
mid-century the conventual buildings and the island were turned over to the
military and the decline of the monastery accelerated with the readaptation of its
cloisters and many rooms to purposes far different from those for which they
had been intended.

Even as recently as the 1920's the church was neglected, the paintings,
many of them masterpieces, suffering from the damp and dust of centuries. A
solitary priest showed to the few visitors the treasures which were there, among
them the two great paintings by Jacopo Tintoretto which flanked the choir.
They had not lost then the dull and viscid varnish which had darkened their
surfaces to obscure much of their pristine beauty. They did not speak then
as they do now, with all the authority of the master's hand.

But a new life and a new energy began to be evident in Venice in the
1920's and the decades which followed. Slowed down in the tragic days of World
War II, this rhythm has been renewed with even greater vigor in the post-war

days. This vitality is in a sense a reflex of the rehabilitation of Venice as a port, in the development of Venezia-Mestre on the immediate mainland; Porta Marghera has become the port for an industrial center of first importance.

Here, then, were the means, but what was imperative was that with the means there should be a desire to make Venice live again in a spiritual sense as a center of studies and intellectual life.

In the 1930's Conte Volpi di Misurata, a great industrialist, one of the major figures in the early development of Mestre and then Secretary of the *Biennale,* the organization which every two years brings the exhibition of modern art and also sponsors many other cultural activities in Venice, presented a plan to the Council with the idea of making San Giorgio again a center of intellectual importance. But the time was not right and the necessary funds to carry out the idea were not there.

However, in 1951 Conte Vittorio Cini took up the idea again and developed it, gave it a new vitality and direction, and with rare practicality brought into being the *Fondazione Giorgio Cini* in memory of his son Giorgio, who had died in 1949 in an accident of aviation. This *Fondazione* was formally constituted by decree of the President of the Republic on July 30, 1951, and with the aid of governmental agencies, the *Fondazione Giorgio Cini* obtained the concession of San Giorgio Maggiore and its island, with the purpose of restoring the monuments and developing there centers of social, cultural, and artistic activity.

73

Conte Cini endowed the *Fondazione* with sufficient funds permitting, under the direction of the Superintendent of Monuments, the restoration of the monuments, which were in a sorry state of decay and desuetude. A congregation of Benedictine monks was brought back as the heart and soul of it all, so that the church again serves its needs. Above all, an organization was created whose purposes were in part social and in part intellectual, thus making the *Fondazione* a practical and working thing in both fields.

The *Fondazione* very wisely did not wish to duplicate institutions which were already existing, wishing to work with such organizations and to implement their activities in every way possible. There was a *Nave Asilo Scilla*, an old Venetian society to give assistance to orphans of sailors and fishermen, founded in 1906, but not incorporated. In the development of the *Centro Marinaro* of the *Fondazione Cini* this was thought of. A section of the island to the northeast was particularly adapted to the society's purpose. For the island has a little port, a *Darsena*, that is a shipbasin, shores eminently fit for workshops and launching ways. It was covered with barracks of the military, of no artistic value, so they could be demolished without any damage to the integrity of the island. Simple but effective buildings in character, necessary for the activities of five hundred boys, were constructed by the architect Luigi Vietti; then the entire complex with all which it contained, living quarters and technical equipment, was entrusted to the care of the reorganized *Instituto Scilla* for the education of the orphans of sailors and fishermen.

74

Extraordinarily complete and up-to-the-moment are all the buildings and machines necessary for proper professional instruction and its practical application. There are examples of all the instruments necessary for navigation, the means of teaching marine biology and ichthyology, natural science and chemistry. All possible equipment is present for the study of carpentry, with all the mechanical aids used in that craft today. There are four launching ways, permitting the actual construction of small boats. There are all the basic technical apparatus for the training of electricians, radio and radar operators, and there are the shops with every modern device, which enables the young man to become proficient not only in the use, but also in the maintenance of the most complicated machinery and equipment. There is a flotilla of school ships: the *Nave Scuola Giorgio Cini*, a naval school, the *panfilo* or yacht San Giorgio Maggiore II, and recently the *motonave*, the motorship Giorgio Cini II of 2500 tons. There is a motorized fishing vessel, *Il Marinaretto*, which can go to sea with thirty students. This is for those who are less interested in technical things, who will no doubt follow a vocation traditional in their families.

Giorgio Cini had a great love for the sea and a great sympathy for those who had been orphaned through the dangers incident to storm and shipwreck, so no service could be more appropriate to his memory. It is truly admirable that these young men can have such an opportunity for practical education and a chance to become useful citizens in a life which more and more requires technical knowledge and ability.

This is only one of the social services of the *Fondazione*. Another is the *Centro Arti e Mestieri*, which is under the administration of the Salesian fathers and occupies the oldest wing of the monastery. This is set up to teach the crafts necessary in so much of life today, the practical things which give many the ability to face the competition for which the unskilled are unprepared. There are courses in carpentry and cabinet-making, courses in many mechanical fields, courses in typography and the many problems concerned with printing, courses in tailoring. The space is adapted for five hundred students, a part of whom are resident, the greater number day students. These services reach quite different needs, obviously, and spread over an extremely wide field the social activities of the *Fondazione*.

But it is the third section, *Il Centro di Cultura e Civiltà*, the Center for the Study of Culture and Civilization, which is the direct descendant of the old traditions of the Benedictines, now living again, and which fulfills in a splendid way the cultural activities that through long centuries made San Giorgio an intellectual center of importance. This is housed in a series of some thirty rooms which include the *Cenacolo* of Palladio, the Library of Longhena, a *Foresteria*, a number of rooms designed to give hospitality to personages in the world of art, culture, and science, a small theater—as well as the exquisite, open-air *Teatro Verde*, the green theater in the gardens, brought to such distinction by the two architects Luigi Vietti and Angelo Scattolin.

Under this section a School of San Giorgio for the study of Venetian

Civilization has been set up under three divisions or *Instituti*, the first for the Story of Art, the second for the Story of Society and the State, the third for the Story of Letters, Music, and the Theater. These *Instituti* have become in a few years important centers of publication for studies in their particular areas.

The *Instituti* are served by a fine Library with a rich collection of photographs, plus a series of microfilms, all of which make it a center of documentation of constantly growing importance, a center which will be increasingly useful to future scholars. The Library is housed in the room designed for that purpose by Longhena, with the monumental bookcases and furniture originally designed for this area by Francesco Pauk. By a happy chance they were found intact. They had been disassembled and removed at the time of the fall of the Republic in 1797 and, fortunately, were in excellent condition and could be secured and reinstalled in their original position.

The island lives again. Palladio's great church has been reordered with an infinite sense of responsibility. The great paintings of Tintoretto have been cleaned and restored. The cloisters have their pristine beauty. The great staircase of Longhena leads to halls which serve many purposes of the *Fondazione*. They act as meeting places for the many congresses and other gatherings which usually convene in the great *Cenacolo* of Palladio. This permits the complete freedom of intellectual exchange which the center fosters.

The gardens have been reactivated and reordered. New ground has been found for their extension by the filling in of the lagoon on the far side of the island. This has given space for properly placing the *Teatro Verde,* the exquisite theater in the open, allowing it to breathe and be surrounded by the plantings which permit its isolation. The theater is there, ready for exceptional presentations possible because of the completeness of its organization and equipment. There, against a background of cypresses with glimpses of the distant lagoon, a company of Greek actors could present masterpieces of Greek drama in a perfect setting.

Unusual opportunities are given to listen to seldom heard music in one of the halls or, it may be, in the setting of the Cloister of the Cypresses. It may be the complete piano works of Chopin played in successive concerts by a master such as Nikita Magaloff, played in the open air under a serene sky flecked with stars and light-filled clouds. The campanile and the dome of San Giorgio profile themselves in sharp perspective. Is this reality or is it, instead, a painted ceiling created by a master's brush?

No, in the Venice of the past, the present lives. As the treasures of her past are projected into a future unforeseen, new values too are created. New trends, new paths are blazed to embrace an ever-widening horizon. San Giorgio takes up again the challenge of the world of ideas.

xiii

FETES AND TRAVESTIES

It is the end of September and the coolness of autumn brings days still warmed by a gracious sun, evenings still warm enough to dine on terraces looking out over a magical lagoon. It is a different public, the mass of indiscriminate tourists has gone. The smart and chic cosmopolitan world of these days is quite different from the world of the cinema, its stars and starlets performing in the stardust of the Excelsior.

No longer is the Palazzo Barbaro taken for a night so that the stars may sparkle for the nonce in their *fards,* their maquillage, their mascara and their rouge under the pitiless lights of the camera they live and struggle for. The triumphant progresses of bosomed cinistars down the Grand Canal, reclame, skywriting against the deep blue of a noonday sky are finished for another year. To a naive spectator, for a moment gigantic letters puffed out upon the heavens had seemed a tribute, too long delayed, to Bernard Berenson, who had honored Venice so greatly in his prose and criticism. But no. Sky-written B.B.'s, fugitive letters of specious and transitory fame, marked instead the progress of a Brigitte Bardot down the length of the Grand Canal.

Katherine Hepburn leans pensively upon a well-curb, a *pozzo,* in the silences of a quiet byway. She looks into the supposititious water of a supposititious well from which the water had departed long since. In a given sequence she steps backward and falls terror-stricken into the waters of a canal. She is pulled out unceremoniously, her hair streaming, her costume hanging in unbecoming flounces about her legs. The next day, due to some ineptitude in the

Maschera su la loggia del Palazzo Ducale, Italico Brass, drawing. The Cleveland Museum of Art, Mary Spedding Milliken Memorial Collection, gift of William Mathewson Milliken.

filming, freshly laundered and starched, she gazes into the same well with the same pensive look, takes the same backward step, and falls again.

The Piazzetta has been taken over for a moment for a film carnival. Gayly colored banners hang from the windows of the Ducal Palace. The light standards of the Piazzetta are masked with a specious colonnade of staff. The space is filled with a semi-brilliant crowd of supernumeraries in masks and costumes. The Doge and Dogaressa disembark from the *Bucintoro* near the *fondamenta* edge. Bright lights focus on them, massed cameras turn their endless miles of celluloid.

Next day a torrential rain has turned the background into the cheap and horrid travesty it really is. The tints of the colonnade of staff have turned a hundred colors. The flags flap unhappily. The hangings from the windows of the Ducal Palace hang drearily, their cheap aniline colors staining the apricot marbles of the palace wall.

The authorities moved quickly: the hangings were withdrawn, the staff columns were removed. But the stains remained for some weeks, causing many a qualm. However, the insecure and fugitive aniline colors quickly faded with the sun. The palace walls regained their pristine coloring and all that was left was a film, a moment's flickering reflection on a silver screen.

Now instead, in these quiet days of autumn, the veritable fetes of other times send their nostalgic memories through the years, projected with a greater permanence. It may be word pictures in the memoirs of their time or

La sfilata dei carri allegorici in Piazza S. Marco in onore dei Conti del Nord, Francesco Guardi, oil. Collection of Count Vittorio Cini, Venice.

Visit of the Pope in Venice: The Pope Greets the Representatives of La Serenissima, Francesco Guardi, oil. The Cleveland Museum of Art, gift of Hanna Fund.

Visit of the Pope in Venice: Pontifical Ceremony in Church of SS. Giovanni and Paolo, Francesco Guardi, oil. The Cleveland Museum of Art, gift of Hanna Fund.

the *aide-memoires*, the scribbles of a Guardi, a Marieschi, a Carlevaris, transcribed in oil or left less permanently upon their handmade papers, in ink, or in pencil or wash, touched with Chinese white.

Mysterious and splendid floats glide around the Piazza di San Marco in procession, honoring the Conti di Nord, heirs of the Russia of a happier time. Guardi's light-touched pencil follows their progress with delight, emanations of a fanciful, if decadent world. The visit of the Pope, Pius VI, in 1782 brought unforgettable moments as well—not forgotten because Guardi, in oil, records the grandees of Venice in costumes of parade as they moved in solemn procession to pay their respects to His Holiness, the Pope, or to assist in the celebration of a High Mass in the great church of SS. Giovanni e Paolo. It is a SS. Giovanni e Paolo which, happily, still retains the choir stalls of its nave.

A Tiepolo does not hesitate to limn in caricature the fleeting aspects of his friends, if that they be, capturing in this way some of the comic aspects of his day. But if he does this, and if these momentary flashes are fascinating, in his grander moments he opens the whole splendor of the skies, the baroque world of supersensory reality. The vaults roll back, and upon the clouds and in the infinite distances of the sky the angels and the saints assist in the splendors of the sacred mysteries.

Canaletto, Bellotto, Carlevaris, Marieschi, each records the Venice of his heart, but each with a different, able, even if pedestrian, hand. But it is aways the romantic aspect of this beautiful and loved city which they project.

85

In Carlevaris and Marieschi it is a more anecdotal world. In Canaletto and Bellotto it is the wonder of an architectural Venice, a Venice which the words of Byron can evoke:

> A faery city of the heart,
> Rising like watercolumns from the sea,
> Of Joy the sojourn, and of Wealth the mart.
> *(Childe Harold's Pilgrimage)*

Caricature, Giovanni Battista Tiepolo, drawing. Collection of William Mathewson Milliken.

xiv

DEATH IN VENICE

The genius of an artist, a painter, a close and very dear friend made of the last rites something of incomparable beauty. "The lady who loved Venice" went to a last rest in her own gondola, served by her own gondoliers. Long streamers of black hung from the *poppa* and draped the sides. White flowers, gladiolas and tuberoses covered the thwarts with their fragrance. *Fiore di Barena,* the flower of the lagoon—a flower which covers the marshes with a purple flush as does the heather on the moors of Scotland when later summer days have come—was a cloth of honor set with the individual flowers of the tuberose, an infinity of blossoms, fragrant, white resting on a bed of purple.

Across the Canal of the Giudecca the cortege passed. The *fondamenta* on either side of Rio San Vio were lined by the few who had loved and served her, and by the many who had seen her pass along the same canal, day in and day out in the bright days and soft evenings of the summer months. It had been a part of the familiar Venice which they accepted without question, and with an instinctive sympathy they said their simple farewell.

The services were over. Friends were present. The waiters from the cafés Florian and Lavena, the custodian from San Zaccaria, the *sarta,* the sewing woman, the women who had come to do some humble and needed service were all there. And faithful Angelo had held the gondola's side, faithful *ganzer,* as he had been for many years.

No, it is not sad to pass on a last journey down the broad waters of the Grand Canal. That canal has seen its days of triumph and its days of sadness, its days of joy and its days of tragedy. The palaces look down upon a changing world. A world of history has passed by them and when an individual goes to his last rest, it is but a moment in a fleeting infinity of time. They honor it with impersonal sympathy, but they honor it in the magnificence of an incomparable frame made by Venetians to enhance life and to enhance death.

No, it is not sad. The passengers on the *Vaporetto* rise, the women cross themselves, the men raise their hats. They have time for simple courtesies. Along the Fondamenta del Carbon and the Fondamenta del Vin there is a moment's pause. Those seated at the tables on the *fondamenta* or on the *imbarcadero,* the landing float at the Rialto, rise. Hats are lifted. The arch of the Rialto frames the last picture.

Across the Sacca della Misericordia, within the rosy bricks of the walls of the island of San Michele, cypresses mass above the waters of the lagoon. Flowers are piled high in tribute. A soul has passed into the boundless spaces of eternity.

XV

MALCONTENTA

Those who, in the early twenties of this century, before the advent of the *autostrada*, took the charming, leisurely, if crowded road along the Brenta from Padua to Venice have some idea of what that region must have been in the days of its glory. Lined with villas, it was the holiday retreat, the favorite place of *villeggiatura* for the Venetian, in spring, in summer, and in autumn. Behind their walls, in the shadows of their trees the villas doze, some inhabited by the families for whom they were built, some reduced to baser uses; some, like the Villa Pisani at Stra, are national monuments, rendezvous of autobus and conducted tour, and rightly so, for few villas can build such a picture of luxurious and sumptuous living which is no more.

Ghostlike among them all was Malcontenta, in those days uninhabited, abandoned, stripped of its trees. It stood stark, desolate, solitary, mirrored in the waters of the Brenta, a nostalgic relic of a past, its sadness intensified by its name and its romantic history.

It was a villa of the Foscari, built here on the edge of the marshes to house a lady of the family whose gracious peccadilloes required a less extensive stage than Venice gave. True or not, the name and the legend, if such it was, seems to have existed as far back as the fourteenth century, and when upon the original site Antonio Palladio built anew a sumptuous summer villa for the Foscari, perhaps the first of Palladio's villas built for a Venetian patrician, the name and the legend lingered in the popular mind.

It was just a few decades later in 1574 that Henry III, King of France, petty son of Catherine di Medici and Henry II of France, was welcomed here. It was indeed a fitting halting place close to the limits of the lagoon, and Henry III was greeted with lavish courtesies, worthy in themselves, but just a tiny hint of the magnificent and splendid festivities which were to mark his reception in the great city close at hand.

Palladio had always sought to give to his interiors a certain monumentality which enhanced life, and this interior, one can be sure, would have enhanced even the stature of that pathetic king, who no doubt enjoyed his moment of respite here before the fatigues that were to come. The plan the architect had chosen has his characteristic clarity and simplicity, a cross-shaped room culminating in a great, vaulted central space, in the four outer corners four ample rooms, an arrangement repeated in less formal fashion on another floor.

Malcontenta in later years had had the good fortune that sometimes comes to those who have achieved a ripe and worthy age. Sensitive and understanding hands have nursed it back bit by bit, with devoted and discerning care, so that the lost beauties show again. Quick-growing trees have been planted to give the necessary landscape background that it craved. The whitewash has disappeared from interior walls, and inch by inch the fascination of the frescoed interior has been revealed again. The villa lives and breathes. It welcomes life within its walls. The great world of Venice comes once more to rejoice in it, to gratify its senses with the joys of music beneath frescoed vaults.

On a mid-afternoon, when the heat lingered, the Boccherini Quintet played the music of Boccherini in the great central salon. The melodies of that music echoing from another century were caught and held lingeringly for a moment within the perfect vaults of that splendid room. There was too brilliant a light at that hour. It fell on tired frescoes with a too searching ray. One could be glad that so much beauty had been saved, but as with those who have passed the first flush of youth, there was a yearning here for a less searching light which would disguise and flatter a bit, hiding the inevitable decrepitudes of time. There was the intermission, gracious refreshments on a lower floor, music again.

The magic hour had come. The harsh light of afternoon had passed. The tired frescoes came out from vault or wall and lived again in all their fullness—frescoes by Battista Zelotti, collaborator of Paolo Veronese, telling of the disgust of the gods at the frailties of man, telling in other rooms of the myths of Aurora, of the earthly joys of Bacchus, of Jove and Giants, of Prometheus.

And Zelotti was there that afternoon. Paolo Veronese walked through and nodded his approval, too. Boccherini took over and conducted his own music. The divine touch of his genius cast over everyone a spell of quiet wonder and delight.

There was a distant rumble of thunder. Dark clouds framed within the lofty portal were flushed with sunset tints. There was a flash of jagged lightning; once more Giorgione's *Tempesta* came to life. And in the witchery of the moment, the gods and goddesses came down from frescoed walls and mingled with the dreams and fantasies of past centuries that had become so very real again.

xvi

DI SOTTO IN SU

Analysis can sometimes wreak havoc upon an idea. On the other hand, what deep pleasure often comes from the realization of qualities which are latent, though unrecognized. A newly found idea can lead the eyes, the feelings into unexperienced worlds of pleasure.

Di sotto in su, the effective Italian way of saying "to look up from below," is a phrase which could have an applicability to Venice and the lagoons. The idea it expresses may be a subtlety hard to put into words, but the idea itself is one to ponder over. It is true, or is it not? It may be a key to unlock another of the many secrets which in their aggregate make Venice and the lagoons what they are.

Venice is quite a different city when seen from the seat of a gondola. There, upon the level of the water, the city literally appears *di sotto in su*. One looks up from below. Even the difference of a few feet gives another character, a different perspective. From a *fondamenta* or a window, Venice is veritably another world. Then it has a more objective personality; the curious, subjective sense of emersion disappears. No longer does the feeling hold of being one with, being identified with, being on a plane with the element which makes Venice what it is.

The subjective identification of oneself with Venice is a curious psychological phenomenon. Through the power of an idea familiar things take on aspects which surprise. Individual impressions enjoyed a thousand times crystallize into new perceptions.

At high tide when the dark line of marine encrustation disappears,

Laguna grigia, Francesco Guardi, oil. Poldi-Pezzoli Museum, Milan.

Venice seems truly one with the seas; stable Venice rides upon the ever shifting, ever moving waters of her canals. But that is the paradox, for the visible world crumbles and the unstable is eternal.

In the open world of the lagoons, the islands are on the level of the eye, covered with the purple *astatici*, the flowers of the lagoon, called in the beautiful Italian way *Fiori di Barena*. The seeds carried by the wind, by the birds have carpeted these salty sand bars touched by the waves. San Francesco nel Deserto seems to float with its dark cypresses and its silences. Across the water the leaning tower of Burano inclines more crazily. The sky has that faint touch of pink with which the painter Guardi defines his blues.

The islands of Torcello rise a few feet with seeming permanence. Circling, Campanile, Basilica, Santa Fosca combine in ever new and ever surprising compositions. Time has left them fringed by the purple of the salt flats. Immersed, cradled by the waves, one with the horizon, the gondola is rocked by the waves on the far-flung and ever moving plane of the lagoons.

xvii

TORCELLO

On approaching Venice from Mestre, the massive Campanile of Torcello is but an indication in the far left, a pen or pencil stroke, a slight brush stroke upon the distant horizons of the lagoon, on clear days fringed with the majestic panorama of mountain peaks, the Alps of Friuli, which bound the flat plains of the Veneto to north and east. It was from the passes of these mountain valleys that the barbarian reached the plains in the faraway days between the fifth and seventh centuries. And while the Roman population resisted as best they could, what could they do, hardly protected as they were by the decadent powers of Rome?

The lagoons of the estuary were close at hand, and fugitives from the incursions of the Huns found refuge there on the islands dispersed in lonely waters. In 638 the Bishop of Altino, pushed by Longobard, brought with him the relics of the saints of his cathedral and transferred his seat to Torcello, the island which, as the years went by, became the central settlement. In the following year, 639, the foundation stone of the Cathedral was laid.

It would be difficult to think how Torcello prospered in those distant centuries, if that memory were not attested by Santa Fosca and the grandeur of the Cathedral. One can hardly believe how rich it was with churches, monasteries, palaces, pleasure houses of every sort. It was the center of flourishing industries, as well, which brought it wealth, prosperity. Only in the fourteenth century did the increasing marshiness of the lagoons in its vicinity, the silting of the waterways, bring days of increasing difficulty. Gradually pushed by necessity, the population transferred itself to other islands, in great part to Venice, and the once prosperous city became bit by bit only a haunting and nostalgic memory, a quarry for the marble and stone needed for the city building on Rialto's shores.

The poor remnant of those who were left was decimated by malaria and the killing fevers of the marsh. Left alone, it became almost a waste land, a land such as Shelley describes in *Julian and Maddolo:*

> a bare strand
> Of hillocks, heaped with an ever shifting sand
> Matted with thistles and amphibious weeds
> Such as from earth's embrace the salt ooze breeds,
> Is this; an uninhabited seaside,
> Which the lone fisher, when his nets are dried
> Abandons; and no other object breaks
> The waste but one dwarf tree and some few stakes
> Broken and unrepaired.

It was early in the present century, however, that the draining of the marshes began to eliminate the malaria and other diseases, so that a better fate has been reserved for Torcello in recent times. A few hardy peasants cultivated the land again, a few vineyards were planted, fields were tilled and the few ruins remaining were made habitable once more. The simple Trattoria of

Attila served their own needs and those of the visitors who came across the long distances of the lagoon in their gondolas to visit the splendid monuments which remained.

With the advent of the little steamboat, the *vaporino*, Torcello became a favorite stop on the tourist route which leads from Murano and Burano to her doors. A landing stage by a tiny canal receives the visitor who comes and who then proceeds on foot, or in *sandolo*, whose gondolier waits to earn the few *soldi* which is their due. Mud banks worn away by the movements of the waters flank the canal; on either side are vineyards, cultivated fields, a simple peasant house in which a graciously arched window reveals a richer past. The *sandolo* passes under the Ponte del Diavolo, an arching bridge without a balustrade, an arch perfect in itself, which gives access to the fields beyond. Then the canal leads directly to the *bacino*, the pool or basin, beside which is the Trattoria, which became the Locanda Cipriani a few years after World War II and has become famous for its culinary treats.

But one is unprepared always for the glories which are in Torcello. The Campanile seen from afar imposes itself more and more as one comes near, but the path, the fields, the canal, the exterior of the Trattoria at the end are rural in the extreme. The Piazzetta has a few simple monuments: a rough marble seat which popular legend calls the "Seat of Attila," a fourteenth century palace of unimposing worth where once the Council of the island held its deliberations, the remains of the Palazzo del'Archivio which houses a museum of a humble sort. Nor does the exterior of Santa Fosca really prepare one, despite the fine ordering of its architecture, with its central octagon surrounded by graceful loggias on five sides, its age-worn and distinguished brickwork, the rich arcading of its apse. The imposing mass of the Cathedral is undecorated except for the loggia along its façade and the distinguished, if simple, decoration of its main portal. But they do not hint of what there is within.

The doors of the Cathedral swing back and as one moves into the interior, the solemn dignity, the majestic proportions, the exquisite decoration of mosaics, marbles—sparse and measured—creates a mood of mystic revery. It does not have the lavishness of San Marco. It has no domes. Instead it is a basilica of pure type. Nine marble columns on each side, with marble capitals of rare loveliness, bear the perpendicular walls which support the open roof of wood, mark and divide nave and side aisles, and move in solemn cadence to the triumphal arch which frames the apse. The Annunciation and the mosaics there prepare for the impact of the central apse below, flanked as it is by a minor apse on either side.

Twelve apostles line the lower apsidal wall. Above on a golden field is the single figure of the Byzantine *Teotoca*, Mother of God.

This solemn and majestic figure upon its mystical gold ground dominates the church, as in the greater richness and elaboration of San Marco no single figure could. Its severe yet gracious lines enhance and enforce the perpendiculars of the side walls, which advance and end effectively in the apse. Its very isolation

99

imposes as few mosaics do: perhaps only the impact of Cefalù may be thought of in comparison.

Santa Maria Assunta, to whom the church is actually dedicated, had guided the steps of the refugees fleeing from the terrors of the plains to seek and to find safety and salvation here, under the beneficence of her protecting hand. The Madonna expresses in an iconographical content the theological ideology of the founding years. Restored, yes, as all mosaics are restored, it has yet retained throughout the centuries the profundity and mystery, the *sfumato* of those years of faith and trepidation.

The church has been restored at various times, in 864 and again in 1008, so that today, in its ensemble, it is typical of the Venetian Byzantine in the eleventh century, though the *Teotoca* brings mystic hints of yet earlier centuries of faith. Below the apse to the left, affixed to the wall, is the inscription IMPERANTE ERACLIO AUGUSTO E PER ORDINE DI ISAACHIO ESARCO E PATRIZIO, the oldest written record—639 A.D.—in the history of the lagoons: "At the time of the Emperor of Byzantium, Eraclio, and by order of Isaac, Exarch of Ravenna."

Of uncertain date, but early, are the exquisite mosaics of the smaller apse to the right, reflecting in various ways the elegancies of the early Ravennate styles. But surely later, twelfth- or thirteenth-century, and more properly Venetian-Byzantine, is the Apotheosis of Christ and the Last Judgment, the vast mosaic which so impressively covers the west or entrance wall.

The eleventh-century pavement with its vari-colored marbles and its patterns leads to the slightly raised choir or presbytery, which extends forward into the nave, before which, to one side, the ambon stands. The choir is probably of the same general date as the pavement, eleventh-century, and the structure of its enclosing balustrades is composed of marble panels carved exquisitely with peacocks, lions, and birds, either addorsed or face to face. In the precinct of the apse rise six high steps, *gradini*, which retain in part their rich covering of marble. The narrow steps in the middle give access to them and to the episcopal seat above. The ancient altar of the seventh century was, happily, reconstructed in 1927, recomposed from original material to replace a baroque structure which was not in keeping with the severe and simple grandeur of the choir.

Upon that altar, almost directly below the triumphal arch, on a summer day in 1939 shortly before the tragic days of World War II, a Solemn High Mass was celebrated to honor the *milletrecentenario*—thirteen hundred years of service to the faith. The clerics of the diocese sat on the curved seats of the central apse. The Patriarch of Venice graced the episcopal seat above. The *Autorità* of Venice, distinguished guests, sat within the presbytery. The church was crowded with those who had come in *vaporino*, in launch, in gondola, or by other embarkations to assist in this historic service of rededication and thanksgiving. As the voices rose in the austere music of the Gregorian chant, the ghosts of other days, of those who through the years had worshipped there, crowded to celebrate once more within these sainted walls the sacred mysteries.

Its Piazzetta came to life again. The Host was carried in solemn procession about its wide spaces, choir boys and clerics bearing candles and filling the air with their chants. The Patriarch blessed the pilgrims gathered there and all the relics of the past which lived again with renewed life. And in the calm and quiet of the evening hours a choir of youthful voices raised aloft its melodies, the ancient and honored music of the Catholic Church: Palestrina, Orlando di Lasso, the Gregorian chant.

That night, one knew well that the ghosts of many centuries pressed close, and as the two gondoliers guided their gondola over the dark and quiet waters, beneath the starlit skies of the lagoon, memories were there which were part of time itself.

It was on a later July day of the same year that Goebbels came in a formal visit to the city of the lagoons. He was received, as was his due, by the *Podestà* and the *Autorità*. The Grand Canal, by order of the state, was decorated with flags, reluctantly, it must be said. But only there, for not another flag appeared in all the city anywhere. Goebbels was honored in the Piazza, too, on a night of *festa*, and appeared on the balcony of the Royal Palace to be received with a minimum of acclaim. He visited the Exhibition of Paolo Veronese in the Palazzo Giustinian several times. But his one request and his chief wish was for a visit to Torcello and for a concert there. Nothing could have been more embarrassing than this. Yet despite the extreme reluctance of the Patriarch, it was finally arranged, and then only because of the international difficulties which a refusal would entail.

It was a beautiful, moonlit night. The music rose again in the softness of the evening light. Its mystic loveliness, a fundamental element in the service of the church, imposed its mood irresistibly. Frau Goebbels wept. Were her tears for the days of faith which were no more, damned by the official atheism of the Nazi creed? One did not know.

But Venice and all Italy laughed upon another score, laughed quietly with the restrained enjoyment characteristic of Italian wit. Every possible courtesy was thought of which would in any way ensure the enjoyment of Goebbels and his entourage. A splendid banquet was prepared. It was in the Trattoria, still called by its ancient name, a name which at this moment seemed to have both a historic and a prophetic cast. It was the Trattoria of Attila, the Hun.

xviii

SAN FRANCESCO NEL DESERTO

To one who follows the footsteps of San Francesco, this island lost in the lagoons is a place worthy of pilgrimage. It has less attraction for the larger public, who in later years go to eat and eat well at Torcello with the culinary excellencies of the Locanda Cipriani, Harry's Bar. San Francesco is not on the tourist route. One must reach it by private motorboat or *sandolo*. But the world has so little time for such simple and homely things; surely it is not a diet adapted to the lightheartedness of Cipriani's world.

For it is truly an island in the far lagoon, suggestive and melancholy with its masses of dark cypresses and pines seen against the southern sky, towards the long line of *lidi,* which divides lagoon from Adriatic. It has no great monuments of art or architecture, only a tiny church with pointed tower, two cloisters, one particularly suggestive of the tranquil loveliness of fourteenth-century simplicity. There is nothing more than the dark cypresses and pines, the ceaseless chatter of the birds, and a legend of surpassing beauty.

In 1220, during a tempest, San Francesco and Fra Illuminato took refuge here when returning from Soria in a Venetian ship. And upon San Francesco's approach the heavens cleared, the sea quieted, and the birds, whose home it was, were silent and listened to the homely magic of his words. And the pilgrim's staff, cut upon the shores of Albania, took root and flourished miraculously so that the barren island became truly a place of trees, a resting place for the sojourn of the birds.

In the simple, rounded apse of the tiny church there was a carved and inlaid reading stand, a humble work, and on it there was a Chorale open wide with music of an earlier mode, illuminated with flowers and leaves in precious colors touched with gold. Here was indeed a vision of Fra Filippo Lippi, a vision of an earlier time, for round it were grouped novitiates who sang as if their very eyes had pierced the skies. They sang because their hearts were glad, their faces glowing with intensity, with a faith which had in it all the happy strength of youth. The older monk who stood close by, worn with many years of saintly poverty, smiled quietly. "They are so young, so earnest. They have just begun the long path that we must follow unto death. Are they not touching in their earnestness?"

The church was silent, but the glad voices had left a memory and a melody in the heart. There was so little to see but so much to feel—the impact of simple piety and faith.

The monk showed with love and understanding what was there. He spoke of San Francesco and his faith. He spoke of how he had preached with such eloquence to the birds. Then he opened a little window that looked out on the inner confines behind the walls. The young novitiates played ball with zest and enthusiasm, their robes tucked up beneath the rope girdle of the Franciscan rule. And all among them were chickens of purple and saffron, bright yellow, crimson, green. The old priest smiled. "They did it all last night. They are so young."

With hearts full, we turned back towards Venice in the gathering dusk.

SAN FRANCESCO NEL DESERTO

Domes and towers were outlined against the sunset light, the Euganean Hills a dark mass beyond the far confines of the lagoon. San Francesco had looked out on skies like this, on distant mountains and the lagoon. The domes and towers were not so different then, and he had heard the age-long chatter of the birds in the dark trees of his retreat.

xix

THE REGATTA

The Regatta is one of the best-loved *feste* of Venice. Its tempo is slow. It has none of the impressive *élan* of the *Palio*, the horse races in the Piazza in Siena. It has no great and overwhelming climax. Yet hundreds and thousands of Venetians crowd the Grand Canal and sit patiently on *fondamenta* or *imbarcadero*, the latter being the landing floats for the *Vaporetto*, the itinerant ferry boat whose regular service is suspended for the afternoon. They enjoy the sun quietly there in whole families or sit for three or more hours in gondola or in one of the various embarkations—the *battelli*, the *peate*, which close the side canals to traffic, the *pontoni* from the Arsenal with their seats for sale, boats whose exact character it is hard for a landlubber to describe with precision.

The entire atmosphere of the afternoon is one of relaxation. It is a *passatempo*, a means of passing the time pleasantly. To the foreigner it seems sometimes to lack verve and spirit, but if he judges it in that way it is with a complete misunderstanding of one of the chief charms of Venice. There is always time in Venice, always has been, always will be. Venice has a genius for spending time simply and quietly, a faculty which a motorized world, adapted to the amenities and the difficulties of land transport and its accelerated tempo, cannot always understand.

The Grand Canal is gay on this afternoon in early September, for a date is always chosen then, after the great heat has passed. *Addobimenti*, the hangings of every description, brocade, velvet, tapestry, or a rug thrown from window or balcony, touch with color the façades of palaces. From them many lean out

Venice: The Regatta, Michiel Marieschi, etching. The Mr. and Mrs. Charles G. Prasse Collection.

lazily, their elbows resting on the red cushions which edge window sills or the balustrades of balconies, these cushions in themselves bringing a touch of color. The individuals chatter, disappear for a moment, only to reappear, for many are the *ricevimenti,* the receptions, given on that afternoon. Hostesses hold open house and the time is passed in pleasant conversation, with the absorbing pleasures of food and drink.

On the canal, too, the itinerant peddler passes by in his bark to sell less delicate confections, beer, Coca-Cola, or one of the other popular beverages of the moment. Others sell *cocomero* or *anguria,* the watermelon so loved and relished by the Italian *popolo.* The family cuts it into bits, distributing it to enjoy its refreshing coolness. The rind then joins the hundreds of other pieces thrown into the canal to be carried by the tide to the Lido's mouth. Thus Venice provides free water transportation for the debris which in our parks and streets would still be litter after whatsoever celebration. A *battello* passes, full of youngsters gay with beer or perhaps gay with excess of animal spirits, who sing the popular songs of the moment or with much hilarity play some stupid trick upon one or more of their companions. The *porcellino,* the pig carefully manicured, passes by in a *sandolo,* safe for the moment in his wooden cage. He is the prize to whoever comes in fourth in the main race. Why this rather dubious prize goes to him who places fourth is hard to understand. Perhaps it is because of the fact that the fourth is the last in the prize money.

At three-thirty or thereabouts the cortege, the *Cortèo,* passes. Everyone

Reception of a Dignitary, Francesco Guardi, oil. Museum of Fine Arts, Boston.

is on his feet in bark or on *fondamenta*. The palace windows and balconies are full. The two great parade boats with twelve and eighteen rowers—called *dodesona* and *disdotona*—moving in rhythmic precision, lead the procession, preceding embarkations that symbolize San Marco. There are ten *Bissone*, gilded and elaborate craft each with eight *vogatori*, the rowers, in elaborate costumes appropriate each to the subject the *Bissona* represents: Geography, the Sea, Byzantium, Fame, Venice, China, and so forth. These *Bissone* are the provocative or evocative confections made expressly for pageants, made with all the showiness of gilding and color which such an occasion demands. They are the attendant ships which accompany and precede the *Bucintoro*, the magnificent ship of state, representative of Venice, the *Serenissima*. Its gondoliers, in colorful velvets rich with golden braid, row to the sound of trumpets and tambours—which are to a more literally-minded audience merely drums. At the stern sits the Doge of Venice and the Queen of Cyprus. Valets stand behind them, flanking a dignitary who holds aloft the bared sword, the sword of state. Attendant embarkations on either side carry the banners of the four great maritime republics, Venice, Genoa, Pisa, and Amalfi. Completing the picture are graciously decorated gondolas covered with flowers, richly caparisoned with silk and velvet. These gondolas hold the *suite*—noblemen with their ladies, ambassadors from the Orient, delegates from Cyprus, accompanied and supported by four of the larger *caorline*. In two, four Moors stand erect, in each of the others, four warriors. The *Cortèo* sweeps the whole length of the Grand Canal and returns to finish before the official stand, the *Palco,* in front of the Palazzo Foscari.

It is all informal and easy. The public recognize this or that friend masquerading in unaccustomed garments and call out delightedly to them. Giuseppe sees his brothers, Anafesto and Giulio, splendid in their costumes on the *Bissona Cavalli,* the two gilded horses of the prow symbolic of the horses of the sea. They wave with the characteristic and attractive Italian gesture of the hand. Their fingers move to them, not away. They say in this sign language, "Come back again," "See you soon, I hope."

It is frankly fancy-dress, carnival. There is none of the complete absorption in the costume, as such, by the personality of the individual who wears it, which one finds in Siena. There, during the *Palio,* the representatives of the *contrada,* the wards, wear not costumes of fantasy, but authentic costumes of the medieval times, and they wear them with pride and authority as if they were to the manner born. In Siena the traditions of the *contrada* and their rivalries still live. Here in Venice there is nothing of that today, the various *sestieri* are mere sections of the city. There are no living and historic rivalries or animosities such as existed in the past between the opposing sides of the Grand Canal, *de citra e de ultra,* on this side or that side, governed by their relation to the Piazza di San Marco. The Regatta is merely an enjoyable pageant meant to delight the eye. It has no deep significance, no profound connection with the inner life of the city.

The first race of the *caorlini* is already underway, the starting place being the Public Gardens, *Giardini Pubblici*. There are nine boats in all, each boat representing one of nine islands in the estuary—Burano, Tre Porti, Cavallino, Lio Piccolo, Massorbo, Sant'Erasmo, Pellestrina, San Pietro in Volta, Vignole. As a boat, these *caorline* are shorter and stubbier than the gondola and considerably wider in their all-over width. For the occasion they are decorated tastefully with garlands of fruit, vegetables, or nets to symbolize the various means by which the individual islands make their living. For they furnish much of the produce which one sees for sale so picturesquely in the markets of the Rialto.

The loud speakers report the positions of the contestants. Lio Piccolo is in the lead. Tre Porti passes. Lio Piccolo regains the lead. Everyone is on his feet as the racers pass by on the long and arduous pull to the turning post at Santa Lucia near the station. Then they return. There is a buzz which grows in volume as the boats appear under the Bridge of the Rialto for the last strenuous bit, the straight-away to the Palazzo Foscari. They carefully play the tide to the full, for it is running strongly. Lio Piccolo maintains its lead and wins.

This race with the *caorline*, each with its six rowers, creates interest and excitement, to be sure, but it is the main race which follows that really holds the public's fancy. Here is a traditional rivalry of champions, a rivalry which has become a highly personalized one. Everyone knows the racers, their past record. The outstanding men are at the oars of the *gondolini*, with them the ablest aid each can find. However, the popular interest is always centered in the personality of the champion himself. He is the one who has given them many a good race in the past in this Regatta or the Regattas of Murano and Burano. He is one of the gondoliers of Venice, a gondolier of the *tragetto*, a Venetian who earns his way ferrying people across the canal when he is not in other service. They know him and he is one of theirs.

The contestants race in *gondolini*, long and slim and low, made in the form of the gondola but much lighter, rowing standing in the traditional manner of the gondolier. Arm bands of different colors single them out and distinguish one from the other. Their names are on everyone's lips. For the moment it may be Fungher, Ciaci, Strigheta. One speaks of Fungher and Ciaci, but the real sympathy is for Strigheta, who has won so many races in the past. Inevitably he has begun to lose to youth, yet his is a strong and proud heart still.

Strigheta is in the lead. He leads as he comes to the Grand Canal, but Fungher, Ciaci pass him there and the race resolves itself into the battle of these three. The crowd roars its encouragement as they pass, follows avidly their positions with the aid of the loud speakers. They return under the Rialto Bridge. This time everyone is pulling for his favorite. Strigheta gains and the noise goes to a crescendo. He all but catches Ciaci, who is second, but he cannot close the gap, and Fungher wins.

The contestants pass. Immediately all boats are in movement, criss-crossing here and there to find their varied ways. The Grand Canal in the direction of the Palazzo Foscari alone is barred to them for a time, closed spectacularly with streams of water from the fireboats. For the winners must present themselves to the tribune at Ca' Foscari to receive their prize awards. With this ceremony, La Storica, the storied Regatta is over for another year, leaving its quota of stories and the rivalries which will be so fiercely renewed at Murano in another year and at Burano in the weeks to come.

Church of San Francesco della Vigna, Luca Carlevaris, engraving. Collection of Italico Brass, Jr.

xx

SAN FRANCESCO DELLA VIGNA

The church of San Francesco della Vigna lies far from the inner life of the city, dominating as it does a quarter which is now one of almost squalid poverty. If one wishes to visit it, it is perhaps as well to go on foot or at sufficiently high tide that the undredged canal will not be a trap to an unsuspecting gondolier. Yet it is one of the great churches of Venice, designed on the plans of Jacopo Sansovino and with a grandiose façade by Antonio Palladio, executed between 1568 and 1572 upon the orders of Giovanni Grimani, Patriarch of Aquileia. Its campanile, placed behind the church, is one of the highest and most impressive in Venice, suggesting on a slightly smaller scale the proportions of the Campanile itself.

The church is surrounded on two sides by an ample *campo,* and its interior is impressive in its simple and gracious proportions, a latin cross with single nave, the choir with altar standing free between choir and retro-choir. The grey of the stone and altar, the light-toned walls give it a harmonious color, enhanced in days of *festa* by rich hangings of crimson damask.

Tombs of the Gritti, of the Bragadin, of the Trevisani, of the Badoer, of Giustiniani, of Contarini and Dandolo are evidence of the place it held in the minds of the great families who made Venice what it was and is. At the crossing, directly before the steps of the choir, deeply cut in the pavement of rose and yellow marble set with black squares, is one of the most impressive of these tombs, one of the most simply elegant of all Venetian tombs. It is a floor plaque with magnificently designed inscriptions which read, OSSA MARC ANTONII TREVISANI PRINCIPIS VIXIT ANNOS LXXIX INPRINCIPATU MDLIIII.

One must pay complete attention to it, for deeply cut in the floor, it is indeed a trap for the unwary. An acanthus scroll ornament, coats of arms of the Trevisani in the four corners, a black band which accentuates the perfect proportions and the magnificence of the perfect lettering—the plaque is nothing more and nothing less than that, but that in itself is worth a pilgrimage.

The church harbors as well one of the most fascinating pictures in Venice, the work of a retardatory painter who signed and dated it "Antonio da Negroponte, 1450." No other work is known by his hand, but there is no one who epitomizes more completely the enchantment of Venice in the mid-fifteenth century than he—a Venice in those days of transition from Gothic to early Renaissance. That the architects of the church recognized its worth and its beauty is evident by the masterly way they framed it in the cool, grey stone of their late Renaissance altar. The color of the stone picks up in perfect fashion and throws into relief the rich architecture of the picture itself.

Antonio da Negroponte sums up the tentative years of a Venice not yet ready for, but turning towards, the Renaissance. It is not the Venice which between 1421 and 1440 had erected the Ca' d'Oro, that palace on the Grand Canal, the perfect expression of the Venetian Gothic. Yet Negroponte still clings to the Gothic in details, and the delicate arcade of his throne has the broken arch of the Gothic, the delicately carved balustrades dear to that taste. But to it he has added the new feeling from Padua, the influences which stem from Donatello and the other Florentines who worked there and which came to fruition in Mantegna. The carved panels of his throne of marble are decorated by Antonio with figures which recall in their form, their foreshortening, and their draperies the antique yearnings of Mantegna.

It is a throne with an intricately designed and curved double platform, with flanking Gothic fantasies of airy balconies and arcades. The central niche with shell is purely Renaissance and not unlike the work of Fra Filippo Lippi, who had worked at Padua. This motive throws into effective relief the Madonna with her magnificent garments of purple and gold brocade, in one of the winding designs which make these fabrics among the most splendid of all time. She sits in hieratic quiet, her hands in an attitude of prayer. She dreams, while an alert Christ Child lies almost casually across her knees. In one hand He holds a sceptre, while with the other He seems ready to clutch the edge of the sleeve of his divine Mother, if need there be.

Fruit hangs from the throne in formal garlands, pears, peaches, apples, apricots, plums, tied with silken cords. Beside the throne and behind is a hedge of pomegranates and rose trees, while on the airy balconies roses mix with pinks, morning glories and zinnias. Everywhere are birds—guinea hen, quail, pheasant, dove, many another—which make a pleasant pattern against the rich ground cover of flowers and leaves.

A great curtain of crimson, hanging from a gilded crown above, is the background in days of ceremony for the high altar of San Francesco della Vigna, massed with candles and white flowers, dividing it from the retro-choir behind.

SAN FRANCESCO DELLA VIGNA

This red and white was the background for a simple faldstool upon which in midchoir sat Cardinal La Fontaine, then Patriarch of Venice. Clad in white, intermediary between the altar and the people, he spoke, spoke with the splendor of his church, yet with a simplicity which reached the hearts of the simplest hearer. He told the oft-told story of San Francesco, told it, it seemed, as if it had never been told before—the story of poverty, of service, of sacrifice, of self-forgetfulness. He told it with infinite simplicity, yet with such an intellectual penetration that, in the telling, he reached not only the mind and heart of the most intellectual of his hearers, but touched and moved the heart and soul of the simplest child. It was truly a sainted spirit speaking, an individual who summed up in himself and in his life all the finest of Catholic ideals, all the majesty and beauty of a church in which he was such a great personality. His was the power of speaking in universal terms, so that not even the least of those within the sound of his voice was forgotten.

The church, filled to the doors with the simple parishioners of this, today one of the poorest parishes in Venice, heard the selfless story of San Francesco. What an experience it was to one who had just come from Assisi, had seen there the celebration of the anniversary of the stigmata, who, Protestant though he was, had attended the midnight Mass in the Cathedral of San Ruffino with the magnificent voices of the Sistine Choir filling that ancient church with the ageless music of the Gregorian chant; who had seen the Host borne in procession beneath its baldaquin through streets lighted only by the thousand lights of candle dips, carried between rows of kneeling thousands through the precipitous streets of that hilltop town down to the Basilica of San Francesco. What a memory it was to one who had, later that early morning, looked across the flat Umbrian plain in the darkness and seen the twinkling wonder of Assisi, lighted from the battlement of the castello, to the Basilica of San Francesco—yes, to the dome of Santa Maria degli Angeli on the valley floor below, lighted with an eternity of lights which flashed then and which will always flash in memory, to tell the story of San Francesco and his devotion unto death.

On that day of celebration and dedication in Venice, in San Francesco della Vigna, one could not help but be overwhelmed by the eternal wonder of faith. To the simple mother with her child who knelt there, as she might another time in some simpler church or in the awesome majesty of San Marco, there was and is always present the inexpressible comfort of belief in a help which comes from above. There may be no sense of the part that the past has played, not even a hint of the miracles of faith which have built San Marco, built San Francesco della Vigna, built the thousand of simpler churches as well. But always present in her heart are the overtones, the unthought-through things, the unexpressed and the unexpressible which have moulded in some subtle way her past and that of her husband, and which will as definitely affect her child.

The congregation in the church with the massed flowers and the crimson hangings of its ceremonial moments, in a service to honor a saint who lived in selflessness and who died having served and saved others, celebrated the eternal sacrifice in the bread and wine, a sacrifice every day renewed. The incense rose in clouds against the crimson background, the candles flashed against the massed white of the flowers. The Chalice was lifted high to be presented to the kneeling people. In that moment of the Elevation, through the side curtains of the choir shafts of light shot through the rolling clouds of incense to surround the uplifted Chalice with a streaming glory. The congregation caught its breath, lifted out of itself in a wave of overwhelming emotion, for they saw in those shafts, and saw rightly, the transcendent realities of the supersensory. It was the stigmata itself. Here was a sign that the eternal wonders are renewed, that, truly, faith, sacrifice for others is a world that ever lives.

xxi

SAN TROVASO—
THE MERCHANT OF VENICE

The *squero* of San Trovaso, one of the shipyards for the repair of smaller craft—*peate, battelli, gondole*—is at the corner of Rio San Trovaso and Rio di Ognissanti. It opens on both of these canals, the launching ways on which ships are drawn for repair, facing in the direction of Rio San Trovaso.

Certainly, it is one of the most picturesque and paintable spots in Venice, a jumble of buildings of considerable complexity, with roofs of red tile, which descend in sharp stages to Rio San Trovaso. The buildings arrange themselves in a rough right angle around the working space, with the broader end on the Rio di Ognissanti. Built of bricks in part covered with plaster, brick from which the plaster has long since fallen, darkened by the vicissitudes of time, it is bound together by additions of wood toned to a deep brown. A *tenda*, a few pots of geranium, clothes hung out to dry add characteristic accents here and there.

Quite in contrast is the other side, the rather severe façade which faces on Campo San Trovaso. It gives no hint of what is hidden there. To be sure, there is the simple but broad balcony seen from the Campo, which runs through and gives on the *squero* as well. It is a simple balcony with a few supports holding a covering of matting, a very minor part, it would seem, in such a picturesque ensemble. Picturesque and useful? Yes. A part of the life of the city? Again, yes. But who would have thought of this balcony as a part of a stage on which a great drama would be played? Yes so it was to be.

A number of plays indigenous or adapted to the Venetian scene were given out of doors in Venice, with the greatest success, in the 1920's. Ready-made for such a purpose, of course, was the *Mercante di Venezia*, Shakespeare's *Merchant of Venice*. But the original and fascinating touch was the idea of giving it in an authentic background of *calli, campi, rii*, which Shakespeare could only indicate in general terms within his text. The *campo*, the small square chosen for this particular presentation was the Campo San Trovaso, which adapted itself admirably to its role. The surroundings became as much an integral part of the drama as the actors themselves. They were not mute sticks and stones but living things which gave an authentic note to the entire performance.

The *Campo* was well suited, being one of the *campi* still retaining the raised central portion which, some say, contained the *cassoni di argilla*, the compartments of clay through which the rainwater passed before entering the central *pozzo* or well which served the area. Others believe that in the early days this section of the *Campo* was a cemetery for the people of the parish, raised for two very sound reasons; first to separate the graves a little and to place them apart from the course of traffic, second to protect them from the depredations of high water. Upon this ready-made platform the audience was seated, facing the south with their backs to the façade of the church. The stage was in part the front section of this raised level. The three steps which lead down join the proper level of the square. On this the greater part of the action occurred. Directly opposite, the sharply arched Ponte di Scoassera with its twelve steps leads to the Calle del Magazen. To the left the stark outer façade and the balcony of the *squero* was astonishingly transformed into the house of Portia at Belmont. To the right the Fondamenta Bonlini along the edge of the canal performed the services of a wing, allowing entrances and exits from that side. It was a simple set, used with much ingenuity and skill. Beyond the canal to the left, a four-storied house with façade of round, arched windows and an iron balcony served as the house of Shylock. The remains of the famous gardens of Ca' Michiel to the far right gave a glamorous touch, a backdrop with pillared loggia above, and a gateway there of elaborate ironwork. It was a proscenium of great effectiveness.

The trumpets sounded and from the right the Prince of Morocco and his suite appeared before the house of Portia at Belmont, to pay court to a Portia played magnificently by Marta Abba, then at the height of her great powers. Graciously received, the Prince made his choice among the three caskets, chose the wrong one, and withdrew. Jessica, dressed as a page, appeared upon the iron balcony of her father's house beyond the canal. In an unaccustomed disguise she waited anxiously, peering down to see if her lover Lorenzo was waiting there below. He showed himself. They met and disappeared.

In Shakespeare's text Shylock's discovery of his daughter's elopement with Lorenzo is merely recounted in the words of a third person, Salanio. Memmo Benassi, however, seized upon it and personified it, making it a moment of overwhelming tragedy. What a figure he made of Shylock, a strange mixture of good and bad, a tender father and a complex sniveling penuriousness and stark tragedy, a sinister figure wrought of revenge and vindictive brutality, yet withal piteous. Whoever saw Memmo Benassi in that part will never forget the desperate dash across the bridge, the frantic "Jessica, Jessica!" the rush up the stairs, the search in every room, the voice fading away, filling the entire square with its insistence, fading away again; then at the last, the breathless and exhausted acceptance of something which he could not as yet believe, his appearance on the iron balcony, the hoarse and gasping cry in which one sensed the utter agony of his heart.

The drama unrolled. Further suitors came to Belmont. The Prince of Aragon, received with restraint and proper courtesy, made his choice and he too failed. Bassanio came, and in her spontaneous rush to greet him Portia revealed in action what she did not dare reveal in words. She froze. She held her peace with vehemence. But when Bassanio chose the proper casket, one knew it was the fulfillment of her heart's desire.

Where but in a Venice with her canals could the Doge of Venice truly arrive in gondola of state to hold his court? Where but there could he arrive with such effectiveness of ceremony? Simply, he held his court framed against a background of crimson cloth, surmounting the twelve steps of the Ponte di Scoassera. Before him, Portia with insistent eloquence pleaded her case, pleaded it, it seemed, as it had never been pleaded before. Antonio was saved.

The scene changed again; a canal at Belmont, a gondola, musicians!

Jessica and Lorenzo floated in truth upon enchanted waters. A full moon hung high in the southern sky:

> How sweet the moonlight sleeps upon this bank,
> Here will we sit, and let the sounds of music
> Creep in our ears; soft stillness, and the night
> Become the touches of sweet harmony:
> Sit Jessica, look how the floor of heaven
> Is thick inlaid with patens of bright gold,
> There's not the smallest orb which thou behold'st
> But in his motion like an angel sings,
> Still quiring to the young-eyed cherubins;
> Such harmony is in immortal souls. . . .

Campo San Trovaso, in some unexplainable way you framed reality that night. Dreams came true. A world came to life. Your pavements and your walls were not mute sticks and stones, but living things.

xxii

SAN ZACCARIA—*LA LOCANDIERA*

Every *campo* in Venice has its own character. A few, however, have
something very special, a beauty enhanced by a way every house, every tree,
everything which concerns it fits into an ensemble. There is in some of these
squares an inevitability, a complete lack of searching for effect, a kind of
ambiance, serenity, which it is hard to put into words.

Of such is the Campo San Zaccaria. It lives its own life. It has its own
indecipherable personality, a sense of life lived and being lived, the sense of
a past and present merged. It is a quiet backwater with a silence intensified by
the very contrast, for it is only a step away from the movement and brashness
of the Riva degli Schiavoni.

The waning light of the afternoon fills with shadow the narrow and
busy Ruga Giuffa di San Apollonia which leads to it from La Canonica behind
San Marco—luminous shadows, to be sure, but the blinding light of noon has
passed. On the Ponte San Provolo and in Campo San Provolo direct sunlight
has disappeared. The stream of traffic funnels sharply to the left. The lines of
the pavement, too, the ways of intense life pass that way.

But straight ahead a shadowed doorway frames a vista, a doorway of
flowered Venetian Gothic surmounted by a bas-relief. The Baptist and San Marco
flank a gracious Madonna and Child who preside with elegance, but reserve.
It is a shadowed entrance from which the pavement breaks and slants away
in sharp perspective to the right to cross a *campo* where the light of afternoon is
filtered into gold, Campo San Zaccaria.

SAN ZACCARIA—*LA LOCANDIERA*

    The church which gives its name to the *campo* flanks the further side. Mauro Coducci, the great architect who completed it, is one of the unsung artists who made Venice what it is. His name is not on the lips of everyone. But he should be better known, as much for his generosity and grace as for his architecture. He took the lower part of the façade and left it as it was, and is. He took the interior, already indicated in its general lines upon the earlier plans of Antonio Gambello, and brought it to conclusion. But Coducci brought the Renaissance with him, in the interior with its detail, and in the façade with its splendid design of blind niches, balanced windows, solids and voids, culminating in the great arch, echoed and supported by curved wings on either side which surmount Gambello's *stilobate* or base. Below in Gambello's design, in the squares and rectangles of rose Veronese marble and white Istrian stone, there are hints of the Gothic of an earlier time, but in the simple abstractions of their geometric design do they not peer into a future, too, these abstractions of an earlier age? But it is the rose color of this base which warms, brings intimacy and homeliness. It is this color, framed by the cold grey of darkened stone, which draws one into this *campo* to peace and friendliness—a balance of warm and cold, the subtlety of understatement.

    But the moment has come. The sacristan waiting by the open door has already removed the candles from before Giovanni Bellini's great masterpiece. He stands by the door with a mirror to reflect the sun upon the painted surfaces, to make relive the glowing colors of a golden time in Venice when the

129

Renaissance came to a new maturity there. Dated 1505, the painting is touched by the magic of Giorgione, fellow pupil of Titian in Bellini's studio.

In a brief span of years Giorgione changed the whole perspective of Venetian art. His early death, before 1510, makes even more poignant his achievements. Youth sparked a vision. For he dreamed dreams, and for a short moment Venetian art stood waiting, hovering on the threshold of what was to be. Youth and age looked into the promised land, full of light, richness, and warmth. Now the atmosphere is shot with filaments of gold. A note of music vibrates in the air, celestial music. It lingers and will ever linger there. For of such stuff is permanence.

The Madonna and Child sit enthroned in majesty before an apse which frames them and gives their figures rare plasticity. An angelic musician draws his bow across responsive strings. San Zaccaria and other saints assist on either side. A narrow, slitlike glimpse of sun-warmed landscape frames the niche on either side and leads the eye away to trees and clouds to a radiant sky.

How many have found an infinity of peace here in the contemplation of this masterpiece? It speaks so to the heart! How many times has a lady sat quietly before this painting in the soft light of a waning afternoon? And where but in Venice would she be remembered still when more than thirty years have passed?

There are unexpected things, too, within the fabric of the church. For to the right a door leads through the sacristy to the Chapel of San Tarasio, the choir and presbytery of the older church of the early fifteenth century. In the Gothic apse the altar of an early time joins with an altar on either side to give a glimpse of a Venice which clung through long years to the rich beauty of her Gothic style. There is the rich elaboration of carved frame which surrounds the colors of pure tempera upon gold, holds them like precious and holy things as if in a reliquary. There is here none of the stupid museum technique of today in Italy which believes that frames, if not original, are out of date, that works of art should stand by themselves, alone, in clinical objectivity. Here frame and picture are a part of that considered whole which was ever in the artist's mind. The stiff and formal dreams of a Giovanni or an Antonio da Murano are ever valued here, painted saints who stand on little pedestals with trelliced flowers and fruit within an architecture of charming fantasy.

Below the main altar are fragments of mosaics of the twelfth century, old pavements of an earlier church, and down a curving stair there is a crypt which, like that of San Marco, dates to the ninth century. When the tide is high the water enters here, for it is one of the earliest of monuments, and like so much of Venice, is gradually sinking into the lagoon with the slow course of the centuries.

Through the years Venice has been gracious to visiting artists, especially in the earlier times before the Venetian artist developed his own strength in the later fifteenth century. Many were called from the outside to assist and were welcomed, too, artists such as Altichiero and Pisanello from

Verona, Gentile da Fabriano from the Marche. There were others who had
worked in Padua in the Basilica of San Antonio. Andrea del Castagno—a name
to conjure with, one of the truly great figures of the early Florentine Renaissance
—frescoed the vaulting of the Gothic choir in the Chapel of San Tarasio,
signed his name and dated it: *Andrea da Florentia-Franciscus de Faventia; 1442.*

World War II fortunately passed Venice by, but it brought deep worry
and a desire for the greater security of her monuments. The conditions of del
Castagno's frescoes seemed perilous. It was not only time, was it not also
the distant shocks of falling bombs which brought about this necessity? For
bombs fell in the lagoon. The *Conte di Savoia,* tied up for long months before
the Riva degli Schiavoni, was only a few steps from San Zaccaria for all this
time. Camouflaged as an island, it had imposed itself in a fantastic and
unbelievable way upon the quiet waters of the Bacino di San Marco. And there it
stayed until in the later days of the war it was moved across the lagoon to the
sheltering trees of the *Alberoni,* trees which suddenly shrank in size before the
immense bulk of this great ship. It could never really be camouflaged. The
Germans in their last despair destroyed it there. Wave after wave of bombers
dropped its lethal load. Flames and eddying smoke made dark for many days the
horizon of the distant lagoon.

In the post-war days a scaffold was built under the apse of this chapel
of San Tarasio. The frescoes of Andrea del Castagno were restored with an
infinity of care. Loose plaster and paint were firmly fixed, repaint removed, and

the precious frescoes appeared anew with a clarity they had not had for many centuries.

What a revelation it is to see the handiwork of a master so close at hand, to see from a scaffold the impact of his brush, to follow the daily stint of his work! Once, in the days before World War II, there was a similar revelation when the ceiling of the Sistine Chapel was restored. There, a hand's breadth away, one could see, could caress the first thoughts and then the finished ideas of a Michelangelo, could see the area of fresh plaster which he painted in a day, could follow the changes he made in an idea sketched in and later slightly modified. Andrea's work is not in quite so happy a condition, but it has its powerful impact too. One can see how the paint of his full brush was absorbed by the plaster, still fresh, to leave in depth a record of his genius. One senses, one sees his thoughts revealed in greatest intimacy, the mysterious essence of a creative soul. So much of that is still there, saved through the centuries.

Twilight brings shadow into the church, but the western light still floods the façade. To the left, closing that side of the *campo,* are the arches of the sixteenth-century cloister, the cemetery of the monks in times gone by, now used quite unobtrusively. Opposite the church are houses, shops, an inn, which bring a quiet vitality. The magnificent *pozzo* in the center of the square once served their needs. Acanthus scrolls crumbling with time form the four corners, and decorating two sides are delicate vases of Renaissance design, their scroll handles giving a note of rare elegance. The other sides show a helmet and a coat of arms.

To the right the older front sits back a bit from Gambello's *stilobate.* It seems to retire still further within the shadow of two great trees which shade that corner of the square, two *alberi esotici,* exotic trees from Malaya, the priest says, whose seeds come perhaps from that far-off peninsula. But in reality they are a type of elm called by the botanic name of *celtis.* The brick front, diapered in its lower part, its color drained with time, softened to salmon and rose, is accented with trimmings of Istrian stone. In the far corner but hardly seen, obscured by the trees, rises the brick campanile, Veneto-Byzantine in style and thirteenth-century in date, one of the oldest which exists. A curving iron fence surrounds this section of the square, a crucifix under a shallow wooden canopy, the bare earth below.

It is a square where the centuries have passed quietly with all their seriousness and complexities, with their comic happenings and their tragedies. It is surrounded by buildings which give it continuity. The past lives with the present here.

At the southern side of the square, with its houses of deep maroon fading to rose, at right angles to the earlier façade, flanked to the left by the two great trees, was a proscenium all ready-made; on a Venetian summer night one of Goldoni's most trenchant comedies was presented here, *La Locandiera,* which can be translated *The Mistress of the Inn.* Goldoni had set the scene of this particular play in Florence, but it could just as well have been placed in the Venice he knew so well. For he was born in Venice, and many of the plays he wrote are actually written in the soft Venetian dialect. It is a gay, if cruel, comedy of love and manners which delighted the public of his time and still holds its sparkle and its vitality.

Mirandolina, the Innkeeper, plays innocently with the amorous pretentions of her guests, the Marchese di Forlipopoli and the Conte d'Albafiorita. But she is more intrigued by a third, the Cavaliere di Ripafratta, who frankly proclaims his complete lack of interest in her sex, deriding at the same time his companions because they show such weakness in this respect. Here is the essence of the comedy. For Mirandolina it is a challenge she cannot let pass by, and with insolent cruelty she gradually breaks down the defenses of the unsuspecting Cavaliere. He falls desperately in love. She plays with his affections, and when she has reduced him to utter misery, she marries a man of her own class before the Cavaliere's eyes. This is the comedy or tragedy; Mirandolina has pursued her vendetta to the end. She is a woman happy only in her power to subjugate. She is a heartless and ruthless flirt who feeds her ego on conquests made.

Here was life as it might have been. Beneath these trees, in this Campo San Zaccaria a touch of true imagination had brought back a time and made it real. For a few hours the frivolous world of the eighteenth century lived here again.

xxiii

CAMPO DI SANTO COSMA—
LE BARUFFE CHIOZZOTTE

A great part of the success of the dramatic presentations in the open air in these years was the choice of the particular *campo* where they were produced, in its appropriateness to the play chosen and in its adaptation to the spirit and character of that play. The rather serious and cold aspect of Campo San Trovaso fitted Shakespeare's *Merchant of Venice*. The warm, friendly Campo San Zaccaria was made for the background of Goldoni's *La Locandiera*. Even with the passing of the years there is still a complete identification of each *campo* with those representations. One always hears the echo of Memmo Benassi as Shylock in Campo San Trovaso, searching in every room of his house for his daughter Jessica. One cannot forget the music of the voice of Marta Abba as Portia as she pleaded the case of Bassanio. One is still entertained and amused by the pretended yet amorous flirtations of Mirandolina beneath the trees of San Zaccaria.

A third play chosen to be produced in another year was the famous *Le Baruffe Chiozzotte* of Goldoni. Could it too find a suitable spot for its presentation? Goldoni writes of this comedy in his *Memorie:* "In my youth I was in Chioggia as coadjutor for the chancellor of the criminal court; and I found myself in contact with that numerous, and noisy population of fishermen, sailors, women who have the street as their meeting place. I know their customs, their dialect, their gayness, their *malizia* and I was able to depict them naturally. The capital, Venice, distant from this city less than eight leagues knew also my original types. The comedy therefore had a flattering success."

136

Goldoni spoke truly, for in its gaiety of scene and in the sharpness and vividness of its dialogue, *Le Baruffe Chiozzotte* will always rank as one of his major comedies.

Chioggia has its own particular pattern, which distinguishes it from Venice. It has a long and broad central axis, straight canals lined by *fondamenta* and filled with a bewildering number of boats of many kinds. There is a network of narrow inner alleys and courts, in many of which one finds the fishing nets laid out so that the fisherman can search for the rents which must be repaired. Chioggia is of the people, intensely lived in, and does not always have the *pulizia*, the cleanliness, which marks most of the *calle* and *campi* of Venice. Its *pescheria* and *erberia* are characteristic and have much the same vitality as the fish market and the vegetable and fruit markets of the Rialto in Venice, only on a smaller scale.

But it was the long, straight canals lined with *fondamenta* which were particularly needed for the *mise-en-scène*. These were found ready-made on the Giudecca. The Rio di Santa Eufemia runs directly from the broad Giudecca Canal to the lagoon, bordered first on one side and then on the other with a *fondamenta*. About half way across the island is the Campo di Santo Cosma. A *campo* without much character, it was chosen because it had ample space to seat an audience facing the Rio di Santa Eufemia, and particularly because the Rio delle Convertite and the Fondamenta della Rotonda e delle Convertite which borders it were on axis and at right angles to it. Thus the Rio delle Convertite became the center of a stage extending far into the distance. Two ingenious revolving stages in the immediate foreground to the right and to the left permitted the presentation of the more intimate scenes. To the left a wooden bridge leads directly from the *campo* to the Fondamenta della Rotonda.

What a magnificent opportunity this gave for a stage setting! The Rio delle Convertite was filled with a complication of boats lying sometimes two and three deep along the *fondamenta*. One behind another, the masts, the booms, the colored sails of the various boats half drawn up or thrown over the booms to dry made a perspective in depth of amazing verity and color. It was Chioggia come to life, and because the population of the Giudecca is in part fisherfolk and one sees so often there the *fondamenta* with nets set out to dry or be repaired, the effect was not forced. Here was color and variety, movement, the perfect background for a comedy which concerns only the life of the people.

Le Baruffe Chiozzotte in its essence is nothing but the picture of the petty quarrels and difficulties which concern a small community which passes so much of its life together in the open. In it Goldoni identified himself in an amazing way with them. There were many, to be sure, who felt at the time that it was lowering the art of the theatre to use dialect. Not so Goldoni. He has used here the dialect of Chioggia, very similar to the Venetian but just enough different to give it comic aspects. Indeed, one of the high moments of the entire comedy is in a court scene. Fortunato the fisherman speaks in such a broad dialect that Isodoro the coadjutor from Venice cannot understand a word. This must have reproduced some of the problems that were brought to him for adjustment, problems which perhaps did not actually warrant a court action. Dialect has always had its comic aspects, and Goldoni in this play has used his opportunities to the full.

Throughout the comedy there is a sense of affection on the part of the author for Venice and her lagoons, a sympathy and affection that was perhaps even more profound because Goldoni was so soon to leave his native city for Paris. The play is full of the latent nostalgia he always had for Venice, which runs like a golden thread throughout so much of his writings.

The play has no important plot, but its three acts are full of comic incidents, brilliant and unexpected turns, surprises. Yet always its naturalness and truth is that which only a great dramatist can give to his material. One does not really have to understand the actual words. The situations have an immediacy, impose themselves and explain themselves spontaneously. Of all the plays of Goldoni, *Le Baruffe Chiozzotte* in its vividness and vivacity has certainly never been surpassed. It was not only one of the author's greatest successes in its own time, but it has retained its appeal through the years.

The audience which saw a brilliant and sparkling representation that summer night could truly go home as Goethe did more than a century and a half ago and say, "Now finally I am able to say that I have heard a comedy."

xxiv

THE *FESTA* OF THE REDENTORE

It is hard for the modern man to picture the horror and dismay, the frantic days of terror, helplessness, and desperation which came in the train of the plague. Today with the advances of medicine and successful research for the bases of infection, such a widespread disaster could certainly be controlled. But then medicine could not cope with it, and the questionable hygienic standards of the time provided ready-made conditions under which pestilence could develop and spread. There were none of the vaccinations and injections to control particular diseases, and one did not carry the various certificates which permitted exit from or entrance to particular areas. Alas, too often because of this lack of barriers the plague was transmitted through the ways of commerce. The terrifying result was that it decimated great sections of Europe.

Venice with its far-flung trade connections was particularly vulnerable. In the first place, her commerce touched not only the entire Mediterranean basin, but also the areas which found their outlets there. Simply to name some of the *fondachi* in Venice, the trading centers of the various nations, gives a fair idea of the spread of her commercial interests—*Fondaco degli Arabi, Fondaco dei Persiani, Fondaco dei Turchi, Fondaco dei Tedeschi,* centers for trade with the Arabs, the Persians, the Turks, the Germans. Only the last two buildings exist today, reduced to far different purposes, one being the Natural History Museum, the other the central Post Office, but their position and size give a clear picture of their former importance. An added fact, Giorgione frescoed the façade of the latter, the *Fondaco dei Tedeschi.* One detached fragment is a ruin in the Accademia today.

In the second place, Venice with her incomparable situation, her unique character, her fetes, her gambling pavilions, her incredible luxury had a universal appeal to the casual traveller as well, Europeans and visitors from the Near or farther East. For added to the appeal of business was natural desire and search for pleasure.

Venice had been decimated by the plague many times in the past. Too often this scourge had spread terror and death among her inhabitants, particularly terrifying visitations occurring as late as the sixteenth and seventeenth centuries. These are memorialized by two of the greatest architectural monuments in Venice, the Redentore and Santa Maria della Salute. These magnificent churches must be visualized in that perspective and with the proper realization that they were thank-offerings voted by the Senate. They expressed in some small degree the overwhelming sense of joy and relief which the people felt in the fact that the dreadful affliction had run its course, thankfulness to the divine powers which had aided them in their time of peril and given them strength to rise again.

The Church of the Redentore, voted by the Senate in 1576, was commenced the following year on the designs of Palladio. It was finished and dedicated to Christ the Redeemer in the year 1592. The second, the Basilica of Santa Maria della Salute by Baldassare Longhena, was voted in 1630 and was finally dedicated to the Blessed Virgin in 1687, five years after the death of the architect. In them Venice can boast of two great masterpieces, one of the high Renaissance, one of the Baroque, each of which records a time of anguish and suffering. Each is, as well, a triumphant affirmation of faith.

There was a further provision in the vote of the Senate for the erection of the Redentore which made it obligatory that the *Signoria,* the governing authorities of Venice, should visit that church on the third Sunday in July. It was this provision which brought into being one of the greatest *festa* of the city and one which still continues, the *Veglia* of the Redentore, held, as the name indicates, on the night preceding the church festival. It lives today as one of the most fascinating and at the same time one of the most characteristic of Venetian popular fetes.

On that Saturday evening all Venice comes with songs and music to the broad Canal of the Giudecca. Embarkations of every size cover the Canal, enormous *peate,* great barges, are dressed with lights and flowers. Long trestle tables are set and families, groups of neighbors and friends celebrate the night with food and drink. Every kind of boat is there, gondolas, the smaller *sandolo,* all illuminated, all decorated, each with a table, no matter how small, heaped with refreshments of some sort.

Here one sees that intimate relation of the Venetian to the sea, his joy in his family and in the waters of his canals, and his search to draw from them release and refreshment in the hot days of summer. It is so spontaneous and natural, an expression of Venetians' dependence upon and use of the waters with which their lives are so intimately connected. For to many of them the boats which carry them in this night of pleasure and relaxation are in others hours their means of livelihood. Music and song are everywhere, carefree enjoyment, release from the burden of the humdrum. *Signori, borghesi, popolo,* all classes of society meet in their various boats on these broad waters in that broad camaraderie of enjoyment which marks the Venetian.

The *fondamenta* which line both sides of the canal are also full. Spectators jam the terraces, which in certain places extend out into the canal. The windows of palace and house have each their quota. All Venice seems to be concentrated on the *fondamenta*, or on the Giudecca Canal itself in that area a bit east of the Marittima to the bridge of boats built for the occasion to join the Fondamenta delle Zattere to the Giudecca shore. Tomorrow that bridge will be black with thousands in pilgrimage.

Tonight the *Galleggiante* floats in the midst of the serried embarkations, a stage lit by a thousand lights, a vision of fairyland. It halts. The orchestra of the *Fenice,* a cast of great singers weave their spell and the thousands are suddenly still.

A single bomb bursts. Then the stars drop down, the sparkle of their colors a pattern of light against the evening sky. Scintillations of light run across the moving waters. Roman candles, rockets, gigantic pinwheels, bombs in unending sequence make the night bright with sound and beauty. A final climax and the sky is full. The Milky Way is displaced and shimmers in falling figures against the distant silences of the lagoon.

The night passes, and as the morning comes, the Venetians move in their embarkations across the Bacino and the broad lagoon to greet the sun from the far sands of Lido's shore.

Church of the Redentore, Luca Carlevaris, engraving. Collection of Italico Brass, Jr.

XXV

THE REDENTORE

On the night of the *Veglia* the Church of the Redentore itself is the backdrop about which the festival revolves. Rising in quiet and monumental distinction near the waters of the canal, the grey-white of the façade is thrown into delicate relief by careful lighting. The rosy brick of the nave and transepts and of the fin-like supports which buttress the nave, the rosy tambour of the dome, the towers which rise like minarets, all count only as darks accented by the perfect line of the swelling dome. Moonlight plays upon its surfaces. It seems to float above in unreality, the understatement of a great architect who dreamed his dream and set it here upon the border of a canal.

The interior, too, in the simplicity of its orders is one of the most impressive of all the creations of Palladio, the grey of the stone showing in light relief against the creamy white of the walls. The red curtains which control the light give a warm and rosy tone when drawn against the southern sun. The effect is beautiful and restrained in normal days but on the day of *Festa*, a great crimson curtain hangs from the golden crown above the altar and separates choir and retro-choir. The flowers of the high altar with the candles sparkle against this brilliant background and the whole interior glows with color.

The interior architecture of the church is accented by a strong cornice below the vaults. Another lesser cornice above the three communicating chapels on either side unifies the entire composition, crowned as it is by the great cupola which soars above the crossing. These cornices serve a charming purpose, for they form an all-important element in the decorations which grace the church at the time of the *Festa* itself.

If, in the months preceding, you should have glimpsed the gardens which lie beyond the church and extend to the open lagoon, you might have been puzzled and intrigued by bearded monks in the brown habit of their rule, sprinkling what seem to be many hundreds of potted plants. For what could they be intended? Could they be decorations for the altars? No. At this time they are, instead, the main decorative feature for the church. The cornices are spaced with them, plants beautifully balanced in decorative pattern. Flowering geraniums, flowering petunias with the added accent of their earthenware pots make a pattern of red and purple and white, accenting the architecture and carrying the festive color throughout the upper part of the church even into the circular cornice of the cupola itself. The grey of the stone and the ivory of the walls are thrown into relief by them and the architecture achieves a new dimension. One could not think of a happier or a more gracious invention.

On this day of anniversary, the Redentore is the center of a multitudinous pilgrimage. The Grand Canal is bridged and all ways bring the pilgrims to the long bridge of boats across the Giudecca Canal, which leads directly to the Church itself and gives easy access to the thousands who wish to join in this day of thanksgiving.

As the sun sets, the Cardinal Patriarch of Venice stands upon the steps and looks out upon Venice. He stands there framed by the magnificence of pillared architecture, a façade decorated with the statues of two patron saints, San Marco, patron of Venice, and San Francesco, patron of this church. The Patriarch raises his hand in blessing and the thousands before him kneel on the *fondamenta*, kneel on the steps, kneel on the bridge far across the broad canal. And, above the kneeling figures is another whose blessing is eternal. The sculptured figure of the Risen Christ crowning the cupola of the church is profiled against an evening sky. In majesty He holds His banner high, as He has done for centuries. He too raises His hand to bless the city below, the beloved city of the far lagoons.